Stone Crosses in Mid Cornwall

by

Andrew Langdon

DYFFRESYAS CROWSOW

PROTECTOR OF CROSSES

Published by the Federation of Old Cornwall Societies

ISBN No 0 902660 30 6

Typeset by the Author

Printed by Troutbeck Press, Penryn

ACKNOWLEDGEMENTS

I would like to express my sincere thanks to everyone who has assisted me in completing this, the second edition of *Stone Crosses in Mid Cornwall*, part two in my Cornish cross series.

To Ann Preston-Jones for all her help in reading through, and editing my work.

For photographs, Ruth Hirst, Ann Preston-Jones, Rob Evans, the late Ken Baker, and the late Mary Henderson.

To Angela Broome, librarian at the Royal Institution of Cornwall's Courtney Library, for her help and assistance and to Collin Brewer of Egloshayle for the loan of material from his personal library collection.

To Kathleen 'Bill' Glanville, Sheila Harper, and Steve Hebdige for information regarding crosses in their areas. To Collin Brewer and Tim Dingle for information about the Higher Fawton Cross, to John Tyacke from the Toronto-Cornish Association for information regarding the Cornish cross in Canada, and to the late Bob Ferrett, my uncle, for the memorable trip to Eastbourne to view the Cornish cross in St Mary's church. To Anna Tyacke of the Royal Cornwall Museum for access to view the St Dominic cross-head at the Museum.

To Viviene Coad, English Heritage Field Monument Warden in Sussex for information relating to the Eastbourne Cross. To Caroline Edwards for help in locating the Tehidy Cross at Stockbridge in Hampshire.

To members of various Old Cornwall Societies who have helped and promoted my work: in particular to Rob Evans, the Federation of Old Cornwall Society's Publication Officer and to John Neale of Launceston.

To the many landowners, who have kindly given me access and made me welcome to view their crosses, and the numerous members of the public who have helped me in my quest to seek out further lost crosses in the Cornish countryside.

And finally to the executive committee of the Federation of Old Cornwall Societies for promoting and publishing this series of guide books.

ANDREW LANGDON
Truro

CONTENTS

PREFACE

This is the second edition of the second book in the Federation of Old Cornwall Societies' *Cornish Cross Series*: it covers an area on the north coast from St Mawgan west to St Agnes, and on the south from the river Fowey to the river Fal. The area includes parishes in North Cornwall, Restormel and Carrick districts: please see the following parish map for details.

In this second edition the author has made many changes, including correcting errors, adding new information received, and in some cases changing views due to his continuing research. Although the page numbering is different to the first edition book, the author has retained the same numbering of the crosses, to give continuity to the series. In addition, two crosses have been restored in this area since 1994 and at least one has been removed.

At the time of going to print there are two ongoing projects, one to make and erect a modern wayside cross in an ancient base-stone, and another to shift a cross to a new position. Please see the stop-press on the last page for last minute details.

The author has endeavoured to retain the same format and page layout as his previous guide books in this series: *North Cornwall* 1992 (2nd Edition 1996), *Mid Cornwall* 1994, *East Cornwall* 1996, *West Penwith* 1997 and *West Cornwall* in 1999. He hopes to be able to update the guide books in the future as new discoveries and restoration projects take place.

This guide book has been produced to give up-to-date information and access details and it is not intended to take the place of any definitive work on this subject, but to compliment it. The comprehensive bibliography at the back of the book lists further sources of information on crosses and any works referred to here.

The guide also gives a brief insight into the reasons why stone crosses were erected, their probable age, style and distribution. There is also a brief note about some of the restoration work carried out by both individuals and societies in this area. The main body of the book is a gazetteer of one hundred and three crosses and fragments. This gazetteer is arranged in alphabetical order of parish, each monument being recorded under its ancient (pre 19th century) ecclesiastical parish, rather than its modern civil, or administrative parish. The majority of these crosses are marked on the 1:25 000 Ordnance Survey maps.

The appendix contains references to a number of additional stones, mostly cross-bases, and a chronological list of recent cross discoveries.

The author has had a great deal of enjoyment and pleasure searching out these hitherto hidden crosses. He hopes that readers of this series of guide books will also be stimulated and inspired by these ancient stones and help protect them for future generations.

MAPS

There are two 1:50 000 Landranger Ordnance Survey maps to cover the area included in this guide book, eight 1:25 000 Pathfinder and four 1:25 000 Explorer maps.

Landranger Series

200	Newquay & Bodmin
204	Truro & Falmouth

Pathfinder Series

1346	Newquay
1347	Bodmin
1352	Perranporth
1353	St. Newlyn East, Indian Queens & St. Dennis
1354	St. Austell & Fowey
1360	Truro
1361	Mevagissey & Tregony
1366	Falmouth & St. Mawes

Explorer Series

104	Redruth & St Agnes
105	Falmouth & Mevagissey
106	Newquay & Padstow
107	St Austell & Liskeard

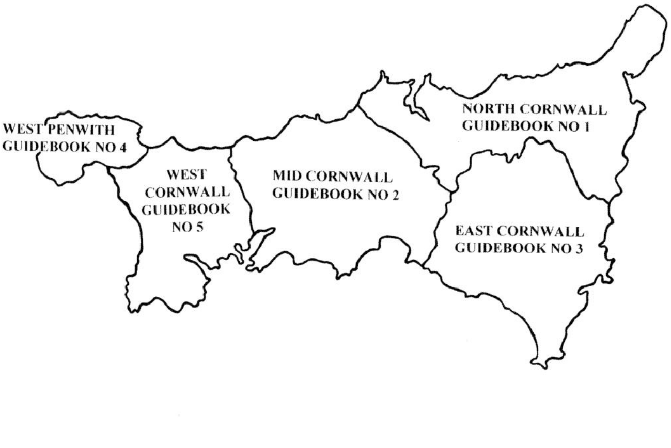

Area covered by Mid Cornwall guide

THE ANCIENT ECCLESIASTICAL PARISHES OF MID CORNWALL COVERED IN THIS GUIDE

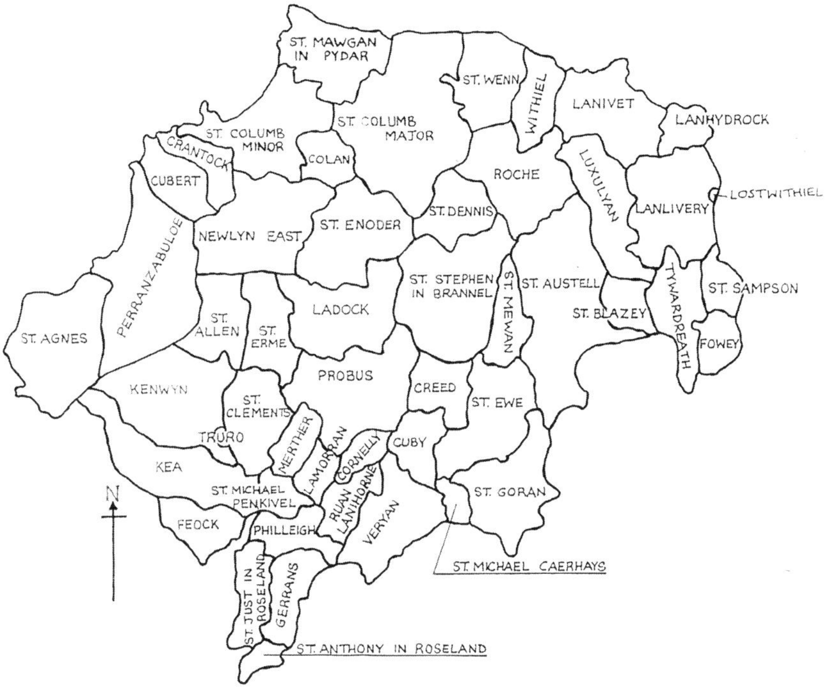

1 - INTRODUCTION

Although there has been a great deal written about Cornwall's ancient stone crosses since the Victorian period, most works are either out of print, or unpublished manuscripts. Moreover, there have been a surprising number of changes to them. That is why this up-to-date series of guide books has been produced: to aid both visitors and residents alike who are interested in these early Christian monuments.

In 1850, Hingston-Randolph was the first historian to publish a book which in part is devoted to crosses. *Ancient Cornish Crosses and Fonts* contains 37 plates of Cornish crosses and although the illustrations are poor by today's standards, it is the earliest record we have for several of the monuments. In 1856 John T. Blight of Penzance published a book called *The Ancient Crosses and Antiquities of West Cornwall* and two years later followed this with a second volume on east Cornwall. In 1872 a second edition combined both volumes under one cover. Many of the north Cornwall crosses were also illustrated by Sir John Maclean in his three volume work on the parochial and family history of the *Deanery of Trigg Minor*, published in 1873, 1876 and 1879 respectively. The hundred of Trigg Minor consisted of twenty north Cornwall parishes and Maclean gave descriptions and illustrations of all the known early Christian monuments and crosses in that area. He also gave an account of the ancient tracks and roads which many of the crosses once marked.

The most impressive and most complete work on Cornish crosses was by Arthur G. Langdon in 1896, entitled *Old Cornish Crosses*. In his book, Langdon recorded 360 monuments, with scaled illustrations of 286 of them, giving a detailed account of their history, style and decoration. He also noted many other Gothic crosses and base-stones and was recognised as the leading authority on the subject of Cornish crosses at the beginning of the century. In 1988 a facsimile of *Old Cornish Crosses* was produced. Although still a most important reference book, at least 130 of the crosses recorded have either been shifted, damaged, renovated or lost since 1896. Langdon also published many additional papers on the subject of crosses, including a chapter in the *Victoria County History of Cornwall* on early Christian monuments, recording crosses discovered since his original work.

During his short life Charles Henderson (1900-1933), perhaps the most well known Cornish historian, continued to discover new crosses. He wrote many additional notes on the subject of crosses, including a supplement to Langdon's work. Later in 1938 a book entitled *Cornish Crosses, Christian and Pagan* was published in which, using many of Langdon's illustrations, T.F.G.Dexter gave a pagan interpretation to many of the monuments. By the 1950s there were many more local historians researching Cornish crosses. Between 1952 and 1968, Surgeon Captain G.E.Ellis published his work on the east Cornwall crosses in the bi-annual journal, *Devon & Cornwall Notes & Queries*. In 1961 Major R.D.Baird and Lady White completed their joint contribution on the Cornish crosses, which in manuscript form was presented to the Royal Institution of Cornwall's Courtney Library. In 1973 Laura Rowe wrote the only guide book on crosses, covering the stones in the west Cornwall area and entitled *Granite Crosses of West Cornwall.*

The most complete work was compiled by Mary Henderson in 1983, who spent an astonishing 30 years on the project. Miss Henderson catalogued over 600 ancient stones, tracing their history through ancient documents and manuscripts. Unfortunately, Miss Henderson's four volume work has not been published but is available, at the Royal Institution of Cornwall, along with a volume of fine pen and ink illustrations by Laura Rowe.

More recently, Ian McNeil Cooke from the Men-an-Tol Studio near Penzance has started producing a limited edition series of guide books entitled *Crosses and churchway paths in the Land's End Peninsula, West Cornwall.* In 1999, he published volume 1 *St Just in Penwith*; in 2000 volume 2 on *Sennen and St Levan* and volume 3 on *St Buryan,* and in 2001 volume 4 on *Paul and Sancreed* parishes. These books, based on individual parishes, give a far more detailed account of the monuments than ever before, reproducing several antiquarian illustrations and up-to-date maps.

The author would like to point out that it is only a coincidence that he bears the same name (A.G.Langdon) as that of the Victorian historian and author of *Old Cornish Crosses.* Similarly, there is no family connection between Charles Henderson and Mary Henderson. For a complete list of further reading on Cornwall's stone crosses, please see the Bibliography.

1i - REASONS FOR ERECTING CROSSES

The county of Cornwall is extremely rich in ancient monuments and antiquities. One of the most numerous of Cornwall's ancient monuments is the stone cross, which cannot be seen anywhere else in the country in such numbers, or in such variety. There are over four hundred complete stone crosses surviving inCornwall and at least another two hundred fragments, with an increasing number of modern replicas. The majority are wayside crosses, set up to mark paths to the parish church, but others were erected on boundaries, in churchyards, or set up as memorials.

a) WAYSIDE CROSSES - The most common type of Cornish cross is the wayside cross which, as its name implies, stands at the side of roads, ancient tracks and footpaths. Its main function was to mark the route to the parish church. In medieval Cornwall, outlying farms and hamlets were usually linked to the churchtown by the most direct route. They would have been mainly single pack-horse tracks, or footpaths, with the occasional cart-track to larger communities. Today these routes are short-cuts to the churchtown and have in most instances become public rights of way, but originally they were the only means of communication. This is why many of Cornwall's public footpaths still go from farm to farm, invariably straight through the farmyard, taking the most direct route to the church. The wayside cross was also used to mark tracks to sites of pilgrimage, monasteries, priories, ancient chapels and holy wells. By the 19th century the county was criss-crossed by many footpaths and tracks forming an elaborate network, which in some cases linked many parishes. It is still possible to walk for many miles in Cornwall on footpaths, without touching a metalled road.

These footpaths were not only used on Sundays for attending church. Several of the mother churches were remote from the centres of population, and in such cases a coffin could be carried miles along church paths, to the church, for burial. An example of this is St Ives which, until the early 15th century, had to bury all its parishioners at the mother church in Lelant, three miles from the fishing port. The chapel did not gain full parochial status until 1576, i.e. it did not obtain the right to perform baptisms and burials, until that time. Therefore, the church paths between St Ives and Lelant must frequently have been used by funeral processions. Some of these footpaths in Cornwall are still known as coffin paths. When the funeral cortege walked the church paths to the parish church, it was usual to stop at each cross so that prayers could be said and for the bearers to take a rest. According to Blight, a cross in St Agnes churchyard was adopted as a lych stone, to rest the coffin on, prior to entering the church (see no 1 in this guide). Again, the church at St Agnes did not obtain the right of burial until 1482, and so before this date all the inhabitants of the village had to be taken to the mother church of Perranzabuloe for burial.

These wayside crosses are predominantly12th century in date and would have been set up during the period when new Norman churches were being built throughout Cornwall. In addition, the wayside cross was also used to mark the main tracks or highways of the day. Wealthy merchants when passing a cross would sometimes leave alms for the poor. This tradition seems to have been revived in some areas: when visiting the North York Moors the author noticed coins left at the foot of several crosses, a practise also continued in Ireland. Many tracks connected priories or marked tracks to monasteries and other ecclesiastical establishments. One such community was that dedicated to St Michael on St Michael's Mount near Marazion, where a Benedictine abbey was established by 1135. On the beach at Marazion there is a rock known as Chapel Rock which, it is said, pilgrims used as the last shrine before visiting the Mount; here a chapel dedicated to the Blessed Virgin Mary stood until 1645. Half-way across the causeway, between Chapel Rock and the Mount, is the base of an ancient cross, still *in situ* beside the causeway. Traditionally, the cross is said to have been broken down in a storm during 1750.

A cross was sometimes used to mark other ancient sites, such as holy wells, chapels and baptisteries. A cross once stood next to the holy well and chapel of St Ia in Camborne parish (West Cornwall no 11), and another cross stands near a footpath to Madron Well near Boswarthen Farm in Madron parish (West Penwith no 73). Crosses were also sometimes placed beside the banks of rivers, to mark a safe fording place. At St Clether on the east side of Bodmin Moor, a footpath crosses the River Inney and a large round-headed cross stands on the south bank, marking shallow water and a firm footing (North Cornwall no 20). The wayside cross was said to guard and guide people to the parish church. The faithful traveller, or pilgrim, would feel secure walking remote tracks in the shadow of the symbol of Christian faith. The monuments were revered and respected during this period, but were later to lose this attention, with changes in religious attitude.

b) BOUNDARY CROSSES - Another reason for the large number of crosses around the Cornish countryside is that the stones were also used to mark boundaries. Crosses were set up to mark parish boundaries and the boundaries of the glebe land. It is also possible that they marked monastic land and even church sanctuaries. Callywith Cross (North Cornwall no 5) at Bodmin still marks the parish boundary between Bodmin and Cardinham. On Tregonetha Downs, a cross known as 'Crossy Ann' stands at the intersection of three parish boundaries ; those of St Columb Major, St Wenn and Roche (see no 97 in this guide). According to Arthur Langdon the Nine Maidens Down cross, which now stands in the grounds of Clowance Estate in Crowan parish (West Cornwall no 31), originally marked the boundary of no less than four parishes. At Cardinham the glebe land was also marked by crosses, four in total, and Rostigan cross is mentioned as a bound stone for glebe land at St Wenn, in a terrier dated 1601 (see no 98 in this guide). In west Cornwall there is less evidence to suggest that crosses were adopted for use as parish bound stones in such numbers as in the rest of the county, although there are a few examples. According to Henderson, a cross known as *Crosse-Keyle* was recorded in the bounds of St Hilary in the 1613 terrier, while stones recorded as *Crous-Sellowe*, near Lambo and *Goen an Grosse,* are mentioned on the bounds between St Erth and Gwinear, also in 1613. On Bartinney Downs in St Just parish there are natural granite boulders incised with small crosses marking the parish boundary, but no free-standing crosses.

c) MEMORIAL CROSSES - There are believed to have been a number of inscribed stones and inscribed crosses in the county, most of which were erected as a memorial to some local king or chieftain. One of the most famous memorial crosses in Cornwall is the King Doniert Stone at St Cleer, which is the pedestal of a fine 9th century decorated cross.

An inscribed stone at Boslow, St Just (West Penwith no 33), which appears to stand on an ancient burial mound, also displays a cross on one face, although there is some conjecture as to whether the symbol was added much later than the latin inscription.

Memorial crosses appear to have followed on from inscribed stones and appear to be more prominent in the countryside in the north and east of the county.

d) CHURCHYARD CROSSES - The most elaborate crosses in Cornwall are usually found in parish churchyards. In many cases the churchyard or burial ground existed before the building of a church or oratory and was known as a *lann*. A *lann* is a raised cemetery or burial ground, usually oval in shape and of great antiquity, as the raised level indicates many centuries of burials. Many parishes still take their names from this prefix followed by the name of the Saint to whom the church was dedicated e.g. Lanhydrock *Lann Hydrek*, Lelant *Lann Anta*. The prefix *llan* in Wales suggests a similar meaning. Some of these crosses may have been erected to mark the Christian burial site, prior to the building of the church. Today most of them pre-date the existing fabric of their churches: for example at Cardinham (East Cornwall no 29).

Inscriptions on some of the churchyard crosses indicate that they were erected as memorials; they may also have been preaching crosses for the early Christians to congregate around to hear readings of the Gospel. The majority of churchyard crosses were impressive monuments and were decorated, rather than plainly carved like the wayside and boundary crosses. There is no evidence to suggest that any of the churchyard crosses in Cornwall are earlier than the 9th century, and most are considered to be between the 10th and 11th centuries. It is quite feasible that during the 8th and 9th centuries carved wooden crosses as prototypes may have been set up, prior to stone examples. The erection of churchyard crosses continued through the centuries: less decorated examples followed during the medieval period but by the 15th century the very elaborate lantern crosses were being set up in some church and chapel yards, for example at St Mawgan in Pydar (see no 67 in this guide) and Lostwithiel churchyard (see no 62 in this guide).

e) VILLAGE/MARKET CROSSES - In Cornwall there are only a few true village or market crosses, although in some cases a wayside cross has been adapted for this function. They were usually set up by the religious authorities, as a reminder of Our Lord, during the day to day bustle of secular life. At Grampound is the remains of a village cross on a stepped base, still one of the focal points of the village (see no 24 in this guide). In the past, proclamations would be read at the village cross and public meetings conducted there. At many of these crosses, merchants sold their goods, thus giving rise to the name market cross. In some English counties these are called butter crosses, from the wares on offer there: as at Winchester; at Salisbury the cross is known as the Poultry Cross. There are records in Cornwall to indicate that at Redruth, St Columb Major and Penryn (West Cornwall no 39) there was a Fish Cross. Taxes and market dues were paid at the cross and the collectors, representing either the Lord of the Manor, or a religious house, occasionally had elaborate shelters built over the cross, to protect themselves from the weather.

Gothic-style structures and canopies, made of timber or stone, usually octagonal in plan can still be seen in many English villages, and even if a conventional cross did not exist, the structures were still known as market crosses. Examples are at Dunster in Somerset and Malmesbury in Wiltshire. At Newport, St Stephen by Launceston, is the only example of a market cross enclosed by a canopy in Cornwall. As the need for larger covered areas on market days increased, many of these structures were demolished to make way for more conventional market halls.

ii - THE DIFFERENT STYLES OF CORNISH CROSS

There are many varieties and styles of Cornish cross, and each can be catalogued by its shape and decoration into one or more main groups. These main groups can also be sub-divided into smaller groups, depending on decoration. Some of the unornamented crosses fit into one main group only, while others can be classified under several groups. The main groups can be defined as : -

a) Cross-slabs and pillars, e.g. In St Columb Major and Colan churchyards.
b) Latin Crosses, e.g. Moor Cottage Cross, Mawgan Cross.
c) Round or Wheel-headed Crosses, many examples in mid Cornwall.
d) Holed Crosses, e.g. St Piran's Cross, Lanherne Cross.
e) Lantern Crosses, e.g. St Mawgan and Lostwithiel Churchyard crosses.

Similarities in style can be found in Cornwall's crosses. The elaborate pre-conquest churchyard crosses appear to have been carved by skilled craftsmen, possibly brought into the local area. Schools of craftsmen may have been set up, especially in Penwith and the Bodmin Moor areas, where distinctive groups of pre-conquest sculpture can be found.

The Penwith group of sculpture features crosses with a figure of Christ on the principal face and five bosses on the reverse face; a central boss and one each on the four limbs. Perhaps the best and possibly the earliest, is the St Buryan churchyard cross (West Penwith no 1); other similar examples can be seen in the churchyards at Paul, Sancreed, St Erth and Phillack, with another which is now in Lanherne, St Mawgan in Pydar (see no 70 in this guide). In the east of the county, we find crosses at St Cleer and St Neot, with similar interlace work, which may be linked to a school which executed the Copplestone Cross at Crediton and another cross which was discovered, built into the Exe bridge, at Exeter.

The medieval wayside and boundary crosses are more parochial in their design. Wheel crosses in the St Clether area are all similar in character, with projections at the neck of the cross and equal-limbed crosses on each face. In both St Neot and Paul parishes the monuments are predominantly of the latin type. Latin crosses only account for about twelve percent of the county's crosses. These crosses would have been carved by the local stone mason in the parish or area and this is reflected in the very local styles. In the Budock, Mabe and Constantine area, most of the crosses display incised decoration, while in the parishes of Stithians and Wendron a group of crosses exhibit chervon-style decoration.

iii - PROBABLE AGE OF CROSSES

The earliest Christian monuments in the county display the *chi rho* monogram, a symbol formed from the first two letters of the name Christ written in Greek: *XPIETOE*. Although this monogram is not strictly a cross, its later stylised form devolves into a cross form. The monogram is found on four inscribed memorial stones in Cornwall and dates from the late 5th to early 6th centuries. Inscribed stones continued to be set up throughout the Dark Ages, some being later converted into free-standing crosses during the medieval period, for example St Clement, Truro (Mid Cornwall no 12).

The earliest free-standing crosses appeared in Cornwall at the end of the 9th century. The Doniert Stone at St Cleer (East Cornwall no 41) is the inscribed pedestal of a cross. It was set up to commemorate Doniert, possibly the Cornish King Dumgarth who drowned in 875 A.D. A cross-shaft in St Neot churchyard displaying similar Hiberno-Saxon decoration to the King Doniert Stone is also considered to be of late 9th century date. The St Just cross-shaft (West Penwith no 25), also displays similar decoration to the St Neot cross-shaft.

Several more churchyard crosses date from the 10th century, including the Penwith group; these are all highly decorated monuments. By the medieval period, except for a few copies of pre-conquest crosses, the majority of the churchyard crosses were much plainer, for example Cury churchyard cross (West Cornwall no 34).

From the 12th century, with the consolidation of the parochial system, with firm boundaries, many wayside crosses were set up. These continued through the 13th and 14th centuries, the later examples displaying chamfered edges to their shafts. Finally, in the 15th century, gothic-style lantern crosses were set up in churchyards (see no 67 in this guide), some of which may be coeval with the re-building of their parish churches.

iv - DISTRIBUTION OF MONUMENTS

Almost ninety percent of the stone crosses in Cornwall are cut from surface moorland granite, and it is therefore not surprising to find that the majority of these monuments are to be found in the moorland areas. The west Penwith moor and Bodmin Moor have the largest concentration of crosses, with smaller accumulations around the Wendron moor and Blackmoor. Another reason for large numbers of crosses in certain areas, was undoubtedly the presence of important religious settlements during the medieval period, such as at St Buryan and Bodmin.

The eastern side of the county, including the parishes bordering the Tamar valley, have few crosses. This area, with the south-east of Cornwall, also has crosses of a much later date. Most are semi-gothic and display either cross-shafts with chamfers, or are octagonal in section. Wheel-headed crosses depicting figures of Christ are found almost exclusively in west Cornwall, although a few have been removed to other parts of the county. Several groups of crosses are found around the two main estuaries on the north coast, the rivers Hayle and Camel. Perhaps this again is partly due to the early Christian settlements, founded by missionaries, from both Wales and Ireland. The author considers that many wayside crosses may have been lost during the early years of Cornwall's industrial revolution, especially in the China clay area, where large areas of moorland have been excavated or destroyed.

v - MATERIALS USED

As previously stated, most stone crosses in Cornwall are cut from some form of moorland granite, usually coarse-grained surface rock. There are however a few exceptions to this. For example, the Lanherne Cross, which formerly stood at Roseworthy in Gwinear parish (see no 70 in this guide) is considered to be cut from Pentewan stone from St Austell and the head of the churchyard cross-head at Breage (West Cornwall no 1), is carved out of sandrock, while a wayside cross in St Clether parish (see North Cornwall no 24), is cut from slate, and the Trelowthas Cross (see no 79 in this guide) is cut from local blue elvan. By the 14th and 15th centuries, materials used in the extensive church building in the county were also adopted for carving crosses. Some of the finest lantern crosses in Cornwall are carved from Cateclewse greenstone, from the coastal quarry at Cateclews Point, near Trevose Head, in the parish of St Merryn. On the south coast, the Polrudden quarry at Pentewan supplied stone for the Lostwithiel lantern cross, as well as a number of fine semi-Gothic Latin crosses in the south-east of the county. It is probable that originally wooden crosses may have been set up, perhaps prior to, or morelikely at the same time as granite ones, in non-granite areas of the county.

Pentewan Stone

The small village of Pentewan (Pentuan) lies on the county's south coast, between St Austell Bay and the fishing port of Mevagissey. During the medieval period several small quarries sprang up on the eastern side of the village, the largest on the Polrudden Estate between the village and Black Head promontory. At Polrudden, a long narrow seam of stone, running north-west, has been quarried from the cliffs inland for approximately three hundred yards. The stone is an intrusive white elvan and its colour varies from light grey to cream or buff. In 1538, John Leland recorded; '*There is a fair Quarre of Whit Free stone on the shore, betwixt Pentowan and Blak Hed*', and later in 1728 John Norden wrote that Polrudden quarry yielded the best freestone in the county. The stone was in great demand during this period for the carving of crosses, fonts and the fabric of many local churches. Records show that Pentewan stone was shipped around the bay to Fowey during the 15th century and up the river to Lostwithiel, where it was taken overland by wagons, to furnish the church of St Petroc at Bodmin.

Examples of crosses cut from Pentewan Stone

There is only one ancient cross worked from this stone and this is the one at Lanherne Convent, which formerly stood at Roseworthy, Gwinear (see no 70 in this guide). This particular monument clearly shows the advantages over granite and the cross is regarded as one of the finest sculptured monuments of the 10th century, in Cornwall. All the remaining crosses carved from this material are of the Gothic period.

Cross Base/Font, St Allen, Mid Cornwall no 7
Creed Lane Base, Creed with Grampound, Mid Cornwall no 23
Market Cross, Creed with Grampound, Mid Cornwall no 24
Fair Cross, Creed with Grampound, Mid Cornwall no 25
Steps of Churchtown Cross, St Ewe, Mid Cornwall no 33
Churchyard Cross, Lamorran, Mid Cornwall no 41
Churchyard Cross, Lostwithiel, Mid Cornwall no 62
Church Porch Cross-base, St Michael Penkivel, Mid Cornwall no 73
Cross-shaft in Churchyard, Tywardreath, Mid Cornwall no 88
Pont Pill Creek Cross, Lanteglos by Fowey, East Cornwall no 54
Polruan Cross, Lanteglos by Fowey, East Cornwall no 55

Other examples of ecclesiastic and secular stonework include at least twenty-five fonts in parish churches; 13th century coffin slabs at Bodmin church; the exterior walls of St Austell Church, the two storey porch at St Petroc's, Bodmin, and the walls of Antony House.

Cateclewse Stone

During the same period, another quarry on Cornwall's north coast was producing stone sculpture of the highest standards. The quarries at Cateclews Point near Trevose in the parish of St Merryn quarried greenstone, locally known as blue elvan, which varies in colour from dark blue to green. The name Cateclewse, according to Charles Henderson, was derived from the words *Carrack-looze*, meaning 'grey-blue rock'. It has been suggested that at Cataclews in the early 15th century, there was a mason of unprecedented talent known as 'the Master of Endellion', who was responsible for a whole series of highly sculptured work in the north Cornwall area.

Amongst the finest work to come from the Cateclewse workshop were the reredos, pieta and stoup in St Issey Church, a tomb in the chancel at St Endellion, along with the tomb of Prior Vyvyan at St Petroc's, Bodmin, and the elaborate lantern crosses of St Kew and St Mawgan in Pydar.

Examples of crosses cut from Cateclewse Stone

Trewane Lantern Cross, formerly from St Kew now at St Neot, East Cornwall no 71
Skisdon Lantern Cross, St Kew, North Cornwall no 44
Churchyard Cross, St Mawgan in Pydar, Mid Cornwall no 67
Bodrean Cross, St Mawgan in Pydar, Mid Cornwall no 69
Tresallyn Cross, St Merryn, North Cornwall no 78
Base-stone in the churchyard, St Merryn, North Cornwall no 77
St Michael's Mount, St Hilary, West Cornwall no 56

Polyphant stone

This is a type of greenstone picrite or blue elvan, which was quarried at the Polyphant quarries in the parish of Lewannick. In the medieval period the stone was extensively used on the ancient buildings of north-east Cornwall, including Launceston Castle and many churches. Although slightly inferior to the Cateclewse greenstone, it was still very popular during this period and was also used to carve more detailed work, such as tombs, fonts, and crosses. The stone varies in colour from grey to dark green.

Examples of crosses cut from Polyphant Stone

High Hall Cross, Laneast, North Cornwall no 52

Other examples of ecclesiastical work using Polyphant stone includes at least 12 medieval fonts, along with fine arcading at Launcells and Week St Mary churches. At the end of the 19th century, Arthur Langdon, author of *Old Cornish Crosses*, designed several modern memorial crosses. These were skilfully carved by Mr F. H. Nicholls of Lewannick using Polyphant stone. Today, examples can still be seen at the churchyards of St Thomas by Launceston, and St Stephens by Launceston.

N.B. The term elvan is a south-western name given by local quarrymen and miners to basic intrusive igneous rock .

2 - THE PRESERVATION OF CROSSES IN MID CORNWALL.

i - Preservation by Old Cornwall Societies. -The first 'Old Cornwall Society' (O.C.S.) was founded at St Ives in 1920, its aim being to record and preserve all things Cornish, such as dialect words, language, traditions, folklore, history and monuments. The Society organised winter lectures and summer pilgrimages and was an immediate success. Within a couple of years several more societies had been formed. In 1924, the Federation of Old Cornwall Societies was formed and in the following year published the first journal, which has continued to be published half-yearly ever since. Today, the Federation boasts 47 societies, all striving to preserve Cornwall's unique heritage.

The area covered by this guide book is represented by twenty different Old Cornwall Societies, several of which have been instrumental in restoring ancient crosses. The Bodmin O.C.S., as well as renovating crosses in St Breward, St Endellion and Bodmin, has also been involved in the re-erection of the Woodley Cross, Lanivet, in 1983 in conjunction with Lanivet Parochial Church Council and, more recently in 1991, the Lamorrick Cross, which is also in the parish. The Newquay O.C.S., to commemorate their 50th anniversary, had the Colan Cross rescued from its use as a fencepost and re-erected in the churchyard at Colan. They have also been involved in the preservation of cross-bases at Trerew and Trevemper in Crantock parish and more recently, repairs to the Treloy gothic cross-shaft at St Columb Minor.

ii Preservation by other groups - At St Mawgan in Pydar, the parochial church council raised £1,500 with the help of its parishioners towards the restoration of their lantern cross. Mr Eric Higgs, together with parishioners from Lanlivery parish, worked relentlessly to re-erect the Trevorry/Sandyway cross, which was stolen from their parish in 1990. Later, in 1991, Mr Higgs' enthusiasm was rewarded when he discovered the Menawink cross, which was later re-erected by neighbouring farmers. In recent years, stone conservators Sue and Lawrence Kelland have been commissioned by English Heritage to restore two crosses in Mid Cornwall, Nancor Cross at Creed with Grampound (see no 26 in this guide) and Trevalsa Cross at St Allen (see no 5 in this guide).

Stonemasons throughout Cornwall have on many occasions been asked to use their skills to restore our Cornish crosses; Truro's High Cross was lengthened by Mr Peter Nottle of Hantergantick granite quarry, while several crosses in the North Cornwall area have been renovated by masons from Tor Down and De Lank Quarries, also at St. Breward. The county also owes a great debt to the workmen from the County Council's Highways department (now Cormac), who have helped to re-erect crosses by the public highways.

iii- Legal Protection - By far the majority of Cornwall's stone crosses are Scheduled Ancient Monuments and are therefore legally protected. Scheduled monuments come under the control of English Heritage and are deemed to be of national importance. If a cross stands on private ground, legally the monument belongs to the landowner, but if the monument is scheduled the landowner will not have the right to remove or damage it without permission from the Secretary of State for the Department of Culture, Media and Sport. If a cross falls into disrepair or is in need of restoration, Scheduled Monument Consent needs to be obtained before any work can be carried out. Protection is also afforded to the area of ground immediately around the monument and below it. Therefore it is also a criminal offence to dig in close proximity to an ancient cross or other Scheduled antiquity, or to carry out repairs without Scheduled Monument Consent.

Some crosses are actually recorded as Listed Buildings and are legally protected and controlled through the local authority's planning department. Sometimes crosses close to historic houses come under the umbrella of the Listed Building that they are close to.

The fact that a cross may be a Scheduled Ancient Monument does not indicate that the public has any rights of access to view the monument; many are still on private property.

In the first instance it is wise to contact the Cornwall Archaeological Unit to report any problems to do with a cross. The Unit is part of the County Council's Historic Environment Service. They can usually advise whether a monument is Scheduled or Listed and what action needs to be taken. The Unit's address is Cornwall Archaeological Unit, Kennall Building, Old County Hall, Station Road, Truro TR1 3AY, telephone number 01872 323603.

3i - DISCOVERING CORNISH CROSSES

During the past twenty years a number of wayside crosses have been discovered throughout the county. Most of these have been found buried head down in the ground in use as gateposts or built into hedges. Some have been exposed when field entrances have been widened to receive larger modern machinery (see West Cornwall no 16), while others have been found when gateposts have been damaged. In Constantine parish in 1993 a wheel-headed cross was discovered due to the erosion of a hedge by cattle (West Cornwall no 29) and in 1991 a cross-head was found buried in the bottom of a garden hedge at Lanivet (see no 58 in this guide).

The ingenuity of the Cornish in adapting these early Christian relics to more mundane secular purposes appears to have been almost unlimited. To a local farmer, a redundant wayside cross was simply a handy piece of stone, and they have been adopted as gateposts, footbridges across mill leats and streams, lintels for fireplaces, door jambs etc. Some were put to more unusual uses, for example as a support for a bee hive, to form a pivot for a horse-drawn threshing machine and their heads have even been hollowed out for use as pig troughs (West Cornwall no 85).

The base-stones of stone crosses were usually of little use to the landowner, as they were normally large boulders of granite with a mortice cut either straight, or part-way, through the stone. Due to their weight these cross-bases were not normally moved a great distance, but were usually pushed up against the nearest hedge and abandoned. Several are built into the foot of a hedge, with their mortice exposed to view, e.g. Trebyan cross-base, Lanhydrock parish (see no 45 in this guide). Therefore, if you find an old cross-base, you can in most cases, be reasonably sure that you are near the site of a cross, marking an ancient track, or boundary.

Today, the discovery of a churchyard cross is virtually unheard of, but during the Victorian period of church restoration, several were discovered built into the fabric of the churches.

Again, during the Victorian era churchyard crosses were sometimes unearthed by the parish sexton whilst grave digging. Today, most churchyards are closed to burials so the likelihood of a cross being discovered is remote. So where do we look? The author always examines gateposts and stiles whilst out walking and has been rewarded on more than one occasion, but it is actually the case that most new discoveries are made by accident - even though documentary evidence to support their positions may be found retrospectively. Field names can also be a clue to discovery: examination of the Tithe Apportionment maps and schedules reveal many field names suggesting a possible cross, for example *Parc an Grouse* - Cornish for 'Cross Field'. Estate maps are also a good source for potential cross sites. The author believes there are still more ancient crosses to be found in the Cornish countryside.

ii - VIEWING THE MONUMENTS

Crosses situated beside public roads, tracks and footpaths pose few problems to the visitor, although some are beside narrow lanes where parking may present difficulties. It is therefore advisable to park at a more suitable site and walk to the monument. In the spring and summer months, crosses built into hedges can sometimes be difficult to locate, due to the growth in vegetation. It is sometimes better to visit them in the winter months when the hedgerows have died back and the monuments are more visible. If in any doubt as to whether a public right of way exists, make enquiries locally; the majority of farmers and landowners are most helpful if approached.

Some of the crosses featured in this guide are preserved in parish churches, many of which are unlocked during daylight hours throughout the summer months. Unfortunately some are now kept locked due to increasing vandalism and theft. In these cases there is usually the name and address of a local key holder, or churchwarden, pinned up in the church porch; the genuine visitor is always welcome. Many crosses remain preserved in the churchyards, where access is not normally restricted unless there is a wedding or funeral service in progress.

There are a few crosses on private estates to which the public can gain access when the gardens are open in aid of local charities (see local press for details). In these cases there is no free access to view the monuments and visitors wishing to see the stones should consult the opening times; charges may apply.

The crosses situated in private grounds are not normally accessible unless a prior arrangement with the owner has been secured.

The author has endeavoured to provide an accurate guide for residents and visitors alike, who wish to view these ancient monuments. At the time of printing all site positions and access details are assumed correct, but the author cannot guarantee these details. Sometimes crosses have been shifted due to the sale of land or property, and a development can in some cases neccessitate the closing or diversion of a public right of way.

iii CROSSES REMOVED TO PRIVATE GARDENS AND ESTATES

Since the beginning of the nineteenth century, the Cornish stone cross has become a 'collectors piece' amongst granite artefacts in the county. During the Victorian period there was an increasing interest in antiquities by local gentry and clergy. This revival coincided with the growing interest in landscaping and gardening, and this lead to many Cornish crosses being uprooted in the name of preservation and set up in the gardens of manor houses, rectories and vicarages. Alongside classical sculptures, summer houses and follies, the humble wayside cross became a focal point in many Cornish gardens.

Today, we would say that the actions of these Victorian gentlemen was perhaps misguided. Many of these crosses were removed from their original locations, with little or no record of their original sites, or date of removal. Once a cross is removed from its original site, a part of its history is lost. In the author's opinion, the history connected with a cross-site can be as important as the monument itself.

On the other hand, it is possible that several of the crosses which are today preserved in private gardens might not otherwise have survived. We have records of many having been destroyed. During the 18th and 19th centuries, not all local people revered them, and some adopted them for more secular purposes such as gateposts, footbridges, lintels and building stones. Some of these crosses were rescued from such a fate, but others may have been better left *in situ*.

Among the private estates which boast stone crosses are four National Trust properties: Lanhydrock, Cotehele, St Michael's Mount and Trelissick, and many smaller manor houses such as Enys, Scorrier, Menabilly, Tonacombe and Lavethan.

iv -CORNISH CROSSES IN EXILE

It was the local gentry and clergy who were responsible for removing our Cornish crosses out of the county. Today, there are at least six crosses which stand beyond the county border, in addition to which one was shipped over to Canada. There are also various notes and references which support the theory that several more unknown crosses suffered a similar fate. In 1991, crosses from the grounds of a manor house on Bodmin Moor were sold, and one has since been removed to the opposite end of the county. These stones could have easily been sold and removed out of the county, a problem that recently occurred in 1999, when the Higher Fawton Cross from St Neot was sold at auction. In this particular case, the sale was not illegal, although today most of Cornwall's crosses have been scheduled as ancient monuments to prevent any re-occurrance.

The author has included the following notes regarding the crosses which have been removed from the county, in chronological order.

A) ST MARY'S CHURCHYARD,EASTBOURNE

This massive monolith was discovered in use as a gatepost on the road between Truro and Redruth, in the parish of Kenwyn. It was acquired by Mr John Giddy from the landowner, on condition that he replaced the stone with a new gatepost. Mr Giddy later gave the cross to his relative Mr Davies Gilbert, author of the *Parochial History of Cornwall* (1838), who formerly lived at Tredrea, St Erth. In 1817, Mr Davies Gilbert had the cross removed to his manor house in Eastbourne. The monument was shipped to London and thence to Hastings, where it was transported by carriage to the manor house gardens at Eastbourne. Here the cross was erected in the grounds on a modern stepped-base by means of ordnance block and tackle. A brass plaque was later fixed to the back of the cross at the neck, which read '*REMOVED FROM CORNWALL MDCCCXVII*'.

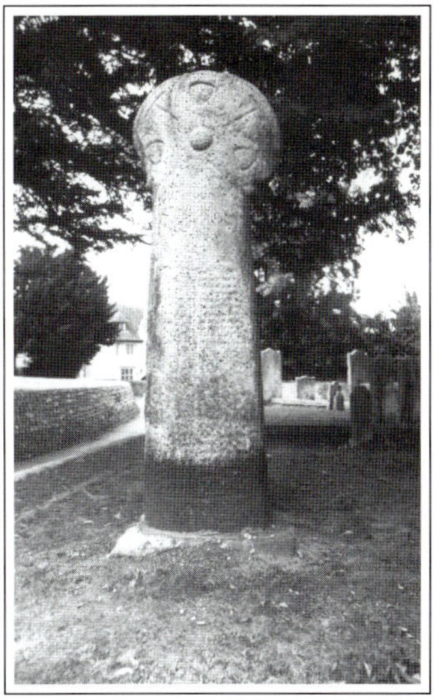

The humorous Mr Gilbert, when questioned as to why he removed the cross from Cornwall, stated, '*to show poor ignorant folk there that there was something bigger in the world than a flint*'.

Henderson suggested that the cross may have been situated near Bosore in the parish of Kenwyn, where there once stood an ancient chapel. In 1922, the cross was again removed and set up in the parish churchyard of St Mary's, Eastbourne, with only the top base-stone. Mr Gilbert's manor house is today the Eastbourne Museum and Towner Art Gallery.

The cross is cut from a grey elvan and its head is oval in shape, rather than circular. The cross-head displays a boss, which is positioned somewhat lower than centre, with three incised triangles and two incised T- shaped symbols forming a unique design on this wheel-headed monument, the reverse face being similar.

The four sides of the shaft are divided up into panels, alternatively plain, or decorated with rows of small holes. Some panels near the base of the cross display incised diagonal crosses on them, while a well defined bead encircles the head and both sides of the cross-shaft.

Dimensions: Height 8ft 2ins (2.49M), width of head 2ft 8ins (0.815M) width of shaft (at neck) 1ft 8ins (0.51M), width of shaft (at base) 2ft 1ins (0.63M), thickness (at top of head) 5ins (0.125M), (at neck) 10ins (0.255M), (at base) 1ft 5 1/2ins (0.445M).

B) FLAMBOROUGH CHURCHYARD, ONTARIO, CANADA

In the middle of the 19th century, while visiting his native Cornwall, the Rev Canon Featherstone L. Osler, M.A. was given two old stones from his brother-in-law, Mr J. H. Hickes of Truro. The stones consisted of a stone cross and a small font. These for many years had lain discarded and neglected at Fentongollan Farm in the parish of St Michael Penkivel.

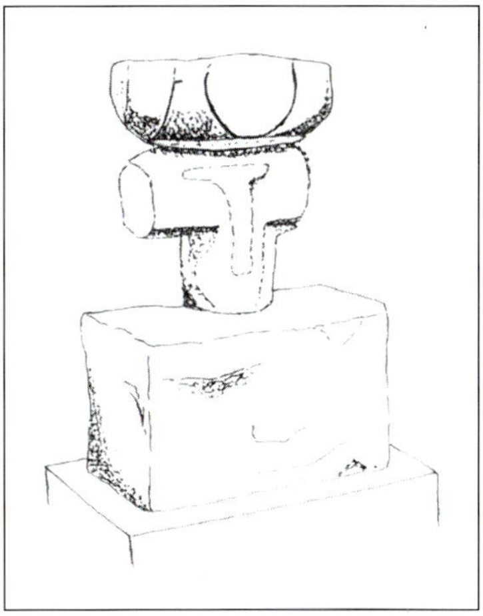

The Rev Osler was at this time the rector of a parish in Ontario, Canada, and on returning to Cornwall in 1837, he removed both the cross and font to Canada. The two monuments were later joined together and set up on a large block of Silurian Limestone from the Niagara escarpment. The composite monument was later set up in Christ Church, in the village of Greensville, West Flamborough. The Rev Osler considered the damaged cross to be a Tau Cross (i.e. T-shaped) of the 5th century. A plaque which is fixed adjacent to the combined monument, states that the font is made up of a bowl and Tau cross belonging to a Cornish church of the 5th century and is mounted to a piece of Canadian stone to form a link between the ancient British and Canadian churches.

On close examination of photographs of the cross and a video loaned to the author by Mr John Tyack of the Toronto-Cornish Association, it can clearly be seen that the stone, although rounded in section, was originally octagonal, suggesting a Gothic style cross. It is therefore possibly a thousand years later than the Rev Osler first estimated. Furthermore, on examination of footage from the video, the author is convinced that the so-called font is no more than a domestic mortar of perhaps 18th century date and clearly agricultural and not ecclesiastical. There is still the remains of a similar Gothic style latin cross remaining in the parish of St Michael Penkivel and also a base-stone, (see nos 72 and 73 in this guide). The latin cross in Canada had formerly been damaged losing its upper limb, which led the Rev Osler to believe the stone was a Tau cross.

C) VILLAGE GREEN, KENTON, DEVON

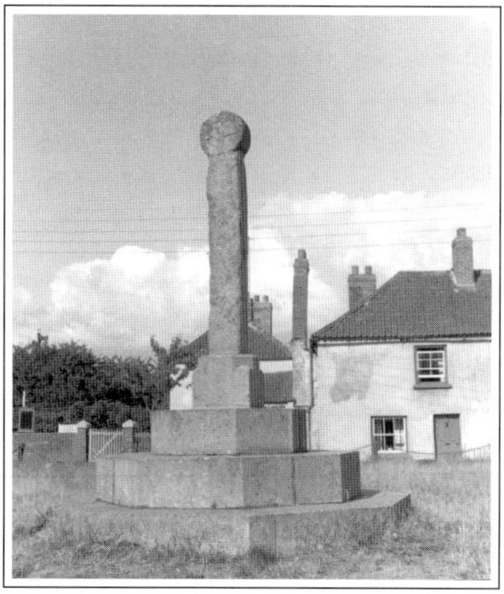

In 1856, a tall slender wheel-headed cross of Cornish granite was brought to Devon and set up on the village green at Kenton, a village a few miles south of Exeter. It was purchased by the 12th Earl of Devon, from a clergyman of an unknown Cornish parish, for the sum of £5 and removed to the Courteney's family seat at Powderham Castle. Allegedly, the cross was later set up on the village green by the Earl of Devon, after the village suffered a disastrous fire. The Courteney family owned extensive lands in Cornwall, and there appears to be no record of the parish from which the cross originated.

Today, the cross is mounted on a modern calvary of three steps, with a new base-stone of Gothic style, which is not in keeping with the ancient monument. The cross-head displays a latin cross in relief, with expanded ends, the lower limb of which extends down the shaft to within a foot of the base-stone. The reverse face displays an equal-limbed cross of similar style on the head. The shaft is plain and has been damaged at some time.

Dimensions: Height 7ft (2.13M), width of head 1ft 4ins (0.405M), width of shaft 11ins to 12ins (0.28 to 0.305M), thickness 9ins to 9 1/2ins (0.23 to 0.24M).

D) HEANTON PUNCHARDON CHURCHYARD NO. 1, DEVON

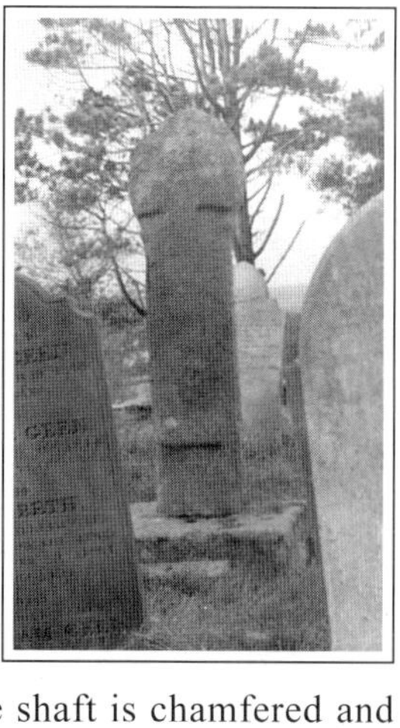

The parish of Heanton Punchardon lies to the north-west of Barnstaple, in North Devon. This cross, along with a second monument (E), were removed from Tregullow House, at Scorrier in the parish of Gwennap with St Day, where they had been brought for preservation. The Williams family who owned Tregullow and the adjoining estate of Scorrier, also had a branch of the family at Heanton Punchardon, and the stones were transported to the parish for adoption as memorial stones to members of the family during the early part of the 20th century.

This wheel-headed cross displays a broad-limbed latin cross with its lower limb extending down the shaft to a horizontal bead, one foot above ground level. On the reverse side is displayed another latin cross, but this time with expanded ends to the limbs, the lower limb only extending as far as the neck of the monument. The shaft is plain except for a similar horizontal bead, again placed one foot above ground level. The edge of the shaft is chamfered and this suggests that the cross may be somewhat later than the majority of wayside crosses, and perhaps a transition towards a Gothic style.

There is no record of the stone's original site, or when the monument was first removed to Tregullow. Henderson suggested that the cross may be the one shown on a map of 1690 as *Crousmenegas* (the Blessed Cross), and situated below Pellyn in the parish of Gwennap with St Day. Today, the cross still acts as a memorial to Sir William R. Williams Bart. 1860 - 1903, and stands on the south side of the churchyard.

Dimensions: Height 5ft 6 1/2ins (1.69M), width of head 1ft 8ins (0.51M), width of shaft 1ft 3ins (0.38M), thickness 1ft (0.305M).

E) HEANTON PUNCHARDON CHURCHYARD NO. 2, DEVON

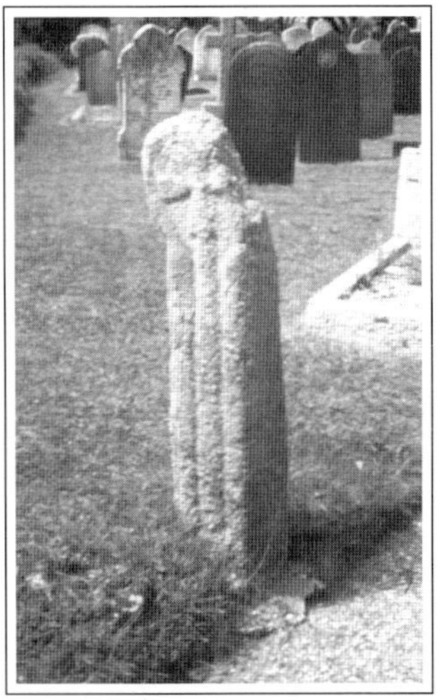

The second cross at Heanton Punchardon is completely different from the first monument and is in a much more damaged condition. In 1850, it was recorded in use as a gatepost near Ponsanooth in the parish of Stithians, and had been removed to Tregullow by the year 1858 for preservation.

The cross appears to have been used as a gatepost without the stone being inverted, therefore this has caused one side of the cross-head and shaft to be cut off to accommodate a high field gate. If the cross had been turned head-down in the ground, as was the usual case when utilising a cross as a gatepost, perhaps the monument would have faired better. Originally the cross displayed a bead running around the head and down both sides of the shaft. Today the cross has lost almost a third of its head and all the beading down one side of the shaft is missing. The cross-head displays an equal-limbed cross in relief with expanded ends, with an incised extension to its lower limb running down the shaft, terminating in an irregular loop. The reverse side of the monument is indistinct and no cross symbol can be identified due to the mutilation of the monument.

In May 1981, a campaign was launched by Mrs R. Ashwell of Ponsanooth, and supported by Miss M. Henderson, to have the crosses returned to Cornwall. This action was strongly opposed by the Parochial Church Council at Heanton Punchardon and no agreement was ever reached. Today, both crosses remain in the North Devon churchyard.

Dimensions: Height 5ft 1ins (1.55M), width of head (originally) 1ft 6ins (0.46M), width of head (now damaged) 1ft 3ins (0.38M), width of shaft 12 1/2ins to 15ins (0.32M to 0.38M), thickness 12 1/2ins (0.32M).

F) STOCKBRIDGE, NEW CEMETERY, HAMPSHIRE

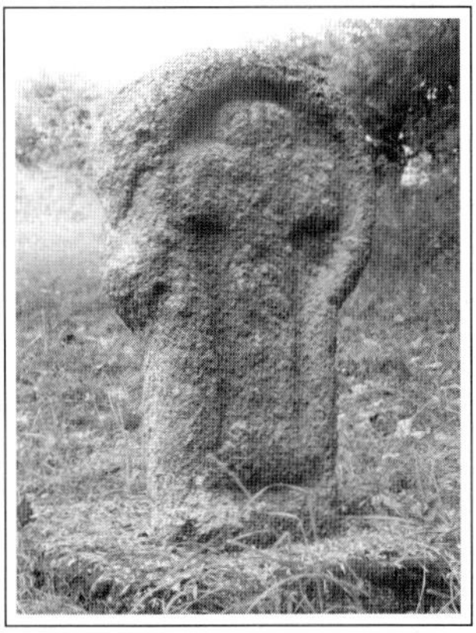

In 1856, this cross was recorded in woods on the north side of the valley at Tehidy Estate, in the parish of Illogan. It was later removed by Arthur Francis Bassett, the landowner, and placed for preservation on the terrace at Tehidy House. In 1916, the Bassett family sold Tehidy and Charles Everitt, the family's agent, was instructed to remove the cross to Henly Manor at Crewkerne, where the family owned a stud farm. Here the monument was viewed by Charles Henderson in 1922, Henderson confirmed that it was still supported by its original base-stone. Eventually the Bassetts sold Henly Manor and moved to Heath House at Stockbridge in Hampshire and the cross was again moved. Here it stood until the death of Mrs Bassett in 1947, when it was removed to the new cemetery at Stockbridge and placed over her grave. It was rediscovered by Mary Henderson, after a great deal of enquiry and detective work. Unfortunately the cross had been badly scarred on one face, due to the addition of an epitaph in leaded letters, which reads; "*In loving Memory of Rebecca, beloved wife of Arthur Francis Bassett, Born 2nd March 1882, Died 27 Nov. 1947.*"

Before the addition of the letters, the monument displayed an equal-limbed cross with parallel limbs in relief, within a wide bead. The reverse face displays a broad-limbed latin cross with a stepped bottom to the lower limb. On this face the bead runs around the head and down both sides of the shaft, completely enclosing the cross. The cross has been damaged on one side of the head, erasing part of the bead. According to Mr Everitt, the agent, the cross was intended to be returned to Cornwall and set up in the churchyard at Illogan, but Mr and Mrs Bassett chose to be buried in Hampshire and the cross remained. A modern copy of a Cornish wheel-headed cross was later brought from Camborne and used for the headstone of Mr Bassett's grave in 1950.

G) ROSKEAR CROSS possibly removed to
HENLY MANOR, CREWKERNE, SOMERSET

The Roskear Cross originally stood opposite Tuckingmill Church and earlier in the 20th century was acquired by Charles Everitt, the agent for the Bassett family at Tehidy. This cross stood in Mr Everitt's garden at Camborne for many years before it was removed to Crewkerne, along with the Tehidy Cross, when Tehidy was sold in 1916.

This was the last time the monument was seen and historians during the past fifty years have frequently been confused between this cross in Mr Everitt's garden and the Tehidy Cross, which he was instructed by Mr Bassett to remove to Crewkerne. It is not known today where this monument stands, nor have we any description of what the cross looked like. The only clue we have is that Mr Everitt died in 1955 in the Reading area. Did he also choose a Cornish cross for his own memorial?

H) CHUTE, NR. WEYHILL, WILTSHIRE
In 1850, according to Mary Henderson, a cross was removed from the parish of St Buryan to Winterbourne, by the Rev Beckerlegge, a Cornish vicar. From here it was later moved again to the village of Chute, in 1900. A bill for the transportation of the monument in 1850 exists, although today the present position of the stone is unknown. In July 2001, the author visited the villages of Upper and Lower Chute, but was unable to gain any information about the alleged monument.

I) WESTMINSTER BRIDGE ROAD, LONDON
The late Arthur Langdon, in his authorative work *Old Cornish Crosses*, recorded that two Cornish crosses existed in the garden of a property on Westminster Bridge in the 1870's, but had recently disappeared (1896). No record of these monuments appears to exist today.

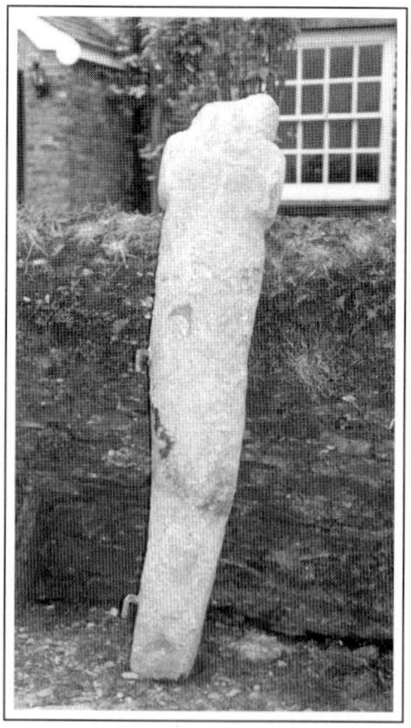

J) HIGHER FAWTON CROSS, formerly from St Neot, now at BLACKAWTON, DEVON.

In 1999, this latin cross was first noticed in a farm sale at Lifton, Devon, by Collin Brewer of Egloshayle. At this time it was not known from where the cross orginated; the auctioneer suggested that in came from near Launceston, but from which side of the border? The cross had previously been used as a gatepost and still displayed iron gate-hangings on the shaft; the author later found out that it had also been auctioned in 1989 with a number of granite gateposts.

The cross was purchased by a private landowner and removed to his farm near Blackawton in Devon. The new owners of the cross intend to erect it as a garden feature on their farm at

Blackawton, although to date, it is still in storage. Later through a great deal of detective work, the author tracked the cross back to St Neot, where it had served as a gatepost on Higher Fawton Farm until 1989.

The author has voiced his concern to the well known firm of auctioneers who sold the cross. This cross may be 12th century in date, and should not be treated in the same way as granite millstones, troughs or staddle stones. The fact that it was discovered in use as a gatepost and was never previously recorded, resulted in it being removed from Cornwall unobserved and unchallenged.

Dimensions: Height 6ft 6 1/2ins (1.995M), width of head 1ft 5 1/2ins (0.445M), width of shaft 10 1/2ins (0.265M0 to 1ft 2ins (0.355M), thickness 9 1/2ins (0.24M) to 11ins (0.28M).

4 - GAZETTEER OF STONE CROSSES

1 Lych-gate Cross, St Agnes
2 Churchyard Cross no 1, St Allen
3 Churchyard Cross no2, St Allen
4 Trefronick Cross, St Allen
5 Trevalsa or Lower Town Cross, St Allen
6 Cross-head fragment, St Allen
7 Cross-base font, St Allen
8 Treverbyn Cross, St Austell
9 Moor Cottage Cross, St Austell
10 Biscovey Stone, St Blazey
11 Latin cross in churchyard, St Blazey
12 Ignioc Stone, St Clement
13 Colan Cross, Colan
14 Base in churchyard, Colan
15 Cross slab, St Columb Major
16 Churchyard Cross-head, St Columb Major
17 Black Cross, St Columb Major
18 Cross Putty, St Columb Major
19 Tregonetha Downs Cross-base, St Columb Major
20 Doublestiles Cross, St Columb Minor
21 Treloy Hill Cross, St Columb Minor
22 Lavethan Cross, St Columb Minor
23 Creed Lane Cross-base, Creed with Grampound
24 Market Cross, Creed with Grampound
25 Fair Cross, Creed with Grampound
26 Nancor Cross, Creed with Grampound
27 Ellenglaze Cross, Cubert
28 Churchyard Cross, St Dennis
29 Fraddon Cross, St Enoder with Mitchell
30 South porch Cross-base, St Enoder with Mitchell
31 Beacon or Corran Cross, St Ewe
32 Bokiddick Cross, Heligan, St Ewe
33 Churchtown Cross, St Ewe
34 Lanhadron Cross-base, St Ewe
35 In the churchyard, Feock
36 Trelissick Garden, Feock
37 Castle Dore Stone, Fowey
38 Gerrans Cross, Gerrans
39 Cross-base inside church, Kea
40 Churchyard Cross-shaft, Kea
41 Churchyard Cross, Lamorran
42 Churchyard Cross, Lanhydrock
43 Treffry Cross, Lanhydrock
44 Bodwen Cross, Lanhydrock
45 Trebyan Cross-base, Lanhydrock
46 Churchyard Cross (north), Lanivet
47 Churchyard Cross (west), Lanivet
48 Bodwannick Cross, Lanivet
49 Reperry Cross, Lanivet
50 St Ingunger Cross, Lanivet
51 Fenton Pits Cross, Lanivet
52 Lesquite Cross, Lanivet
53 Treliggan Cross, Lanivet
54 Lannival Cross, Lanivet
55 Tremore Cross, Lanivet
56 Woodley Cross, Lanivet
57 St Benet's Cross, Lanivet
58 Lamorrick Cross, Lanivet
59 Trethew Cross, Lanlivery
60 Trevorry or Sandyway Cross, Lanlivery
61 Menawink Cross, Lanlivery
62 Churchyard Cross, Lostwithiel
63 Crewel Cross, Lostwithiel
64 Three Stiles Cross, Luxulyan
65 Trevellan Cross, Luxulyan
66 Tregonning Cross-head, Luxulyan
67 Churchyard Cross, St Mawgan in Pydar
68 Mawgan Cross, St Mawgan in Pydar
69 Bodrean Cross, St Mawgan in Pydar
70 Lanherne Cross, St Mawgan in Pydar
71 Tresillian Cross, Merther
72 Fentongollan Cross, St Michael Penkivel
73 Church porch Cross-base, St Michael Penkivel
74a Churchyard Cross, Newlyn East
74b Base of Churchyard cross, Newlyn East
75 Neeham Cross-base, Newlyn East
76 St Piran's Cross, Perranzabuloe
77 Nansmellyn Cross, Perranzabuloe
78 St Piran's Oratory Cross, Perranzabuloe
79 Trelowthas Cross, Probus
80 Churchyard Cross, Roche
81 Glebe Cross, Roche
82 Trerank Cross, Roche
83 Old Rectory Cross, Ruan Lanihorne
84 Churchyard Cross, St Stephen in Brannel
85 Treneague Cross, St Stephen in Brannel
86a St Dominick Street Cross-head, St Mary's Truro
86b High Cross, St Mary's Truro
87 Tretheras Reliquary Cross-head, St Mary's Truro
88 Cross-shaft in churchyard, Tywardreath
89 Tregaminion no 1, Tywardreath
90 Tregaminion no 2, Tywardreath
91 Methrose Cross, Menabilly, Tywardreath
92 Barrs Cross, Menabilly, Tywardreath
93 Trenython Cross, Tywardreath
94 Cross-head in porch wall, Veryan
95 Veryan Cross fragment, Veryan
96 Vicarage Cross, Veryan
97 Crossy Ann, St Wenn
98 Rostigan Cross-shaft, St Wenn
99 Tregurtha Cross-head, St Wenn
100 Rectory Cross, Withiel
101 Inches Cross, Withiel

1

Lych-gate Cross or Lych-stone Cross St Agnes

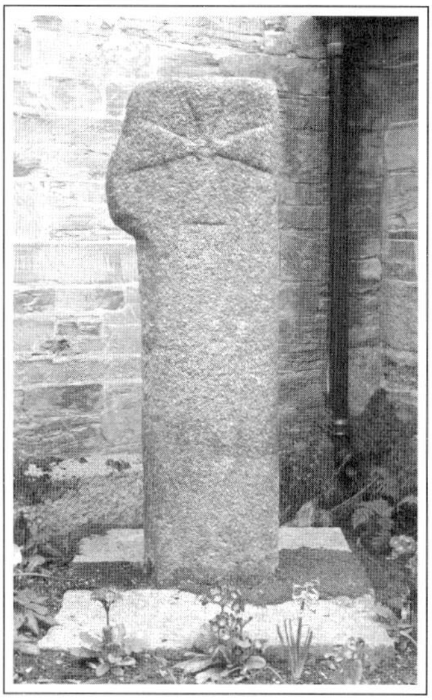

WHEEL-HEADED WAYSIDE CROSS

SX 7203 5073 - Stands on the left-hand side of the south porch of the parish church. St Agnes is situated 9 miles north-west of Truro. Access - Unlimited.

Blight recorded that this mutilated wheel-headed cross was previously used as a Lych-stone, to rest a coffin, before a funeral cortege entered the church. It formerly stood outside the churchyard on the right-hand side of the church gates, and was probably moved in 1935 when the lych-gate was built. On re-examination of this cross, the author considers that it may have previously been re-used as a building stone.

The head displays an equal-limbed cross with expanded ends in relief, on each face. The sharpness of the cross-limbs on the principle face suggests that the cross on this face may have been re-cut. The cross-shaft only has chamfers on two sides, which may suggest that this decoration was added later, perhaps when the cross-head was mutilated. The monument has the appearance of a wayside cross, and probably originally marked a church path somewhere in the parish.

Height 5ft (1.525M), width of head 1ft 8ins (0.51M), width of head (originally) 1ft 10ins (0.56M), width of shaft (at neck) 1ft 4ins (0.405M), width of shaft (at base) 1ft 2 1/2ins (0.37M), thickness 10ins to 12 1/2ins (0.255 to 0.32M) .

2

Churchyard Cross no 1 St Allen

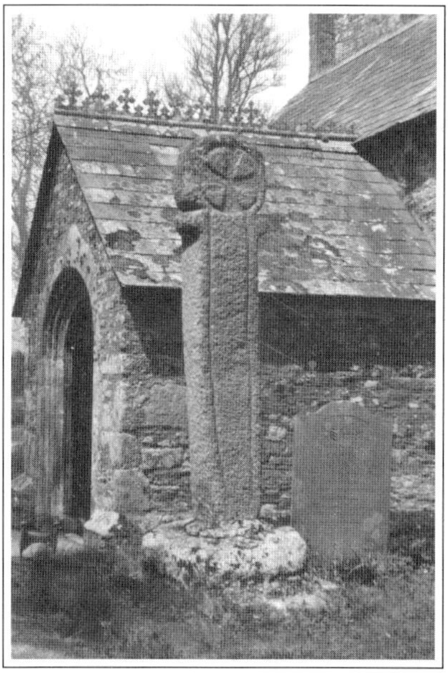

WHEEL-HEADED WAYSIDE CROSS

SW 8225 5060 - On the eastern side of the south porch at St Allen churchyard. St Allen is situated 4 1/2 miles north of the city of Truro. Access - Unlimited.

This well proportioned cross was discovered by the Rev R. L. Glover in 1928 and recorded by Charles Henderson in the Cornish Annual 'Tre Pol Pen' in that year. Later, in 1930, it was re-erected outside the south porch of the parish church close to where it was found. An equal-limbed cross is displayed on each face of the monument, the limbs of which are formed by triangular depressions cut into the stone and enclosed in a bead. At the neck of the cross can be seen small projections; a feature found on many Cornish crosses, especially in the Davidstow/ St Clether areas of the county. On the shaft, which has a marked entasis, is a well defined bead, running down each side from the neck to the base. The base is made up of two circular stones of different diameters: the upper appears to be the original base-stone and the lower is the base of an old cider press. The cross is similar in style to the Trevalsa Cross (see no 5 in this guide).

Height 6ft 3ins (1.91M), width of shaft (at neck) 1ft 1ins (0.33M), width of shaft (at base) 11ins (0.28M), width across projections 1ft 6ins (0.46M), thickness of shaft 7 1/2ins (0.19M), upper base-stone height 7ins (0.18M) , lower base stone dia. 3ft 5ins (1.4M) upper base-stone dia. 2ft 7ins (0.79M).

3

Churchyard Cross no 2
St Allen

WHEEL-HEADED WAYSIDE CROSS

SW 8226 5059 - On the south-eastern side of St Allen churchyard. Access - Unlimited.

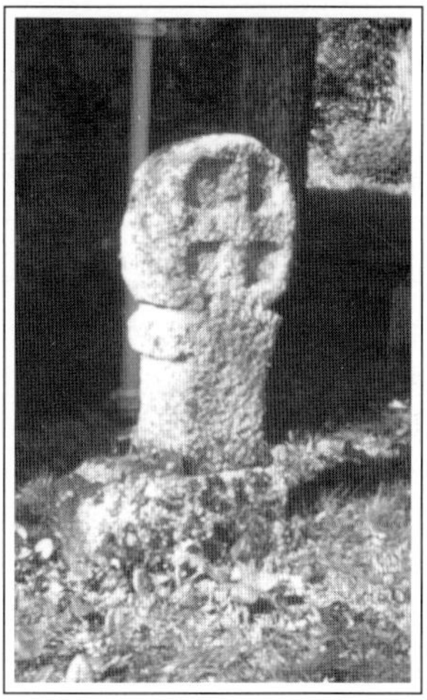

Again, this monument was discovered buried in the churchyard at St Allen. It was discovered in 1862 by the sexton whilst digging a grave for the wife of the rector, the Rev George Morris, below the eastern window of the church. The remains of a gothic latin cross were found at the same time (see no 6 in this guide). The monument was re-erected on a modern base-stone in 1912, due to the efforts of a Mr and Mrs L. Buck.

The head displays an equal-limbed cross on one face, with a fine broad-limbed latin cross on the reverse side, the lower limb of which is extended down the shaft. Each side of the head has a bead enclosing the cross, although it is slightly damaged at the top. The monument has wide projections at the neck and the shaft tapers downwards towards the base-stone. All three of the crosses in St Allen churchyard are coated in thick lichen, which camouflages some of the stones' detail.

Height 2ft 6ins (0.76M) , width at projections 1ft 3ins (0.38M), width of head 1ft 5 1/2ins (0.445M) , width of shaft (at neck) 10ins (0.255M), thickness 8 1/2ins (0.215M).

4

Trefronick Cross
St Allen

WHEEL-HEADED WAYSIDE CROSS

SW 8223 5060 - Near the south-west angle of the parish church.
Access - Unlimited.

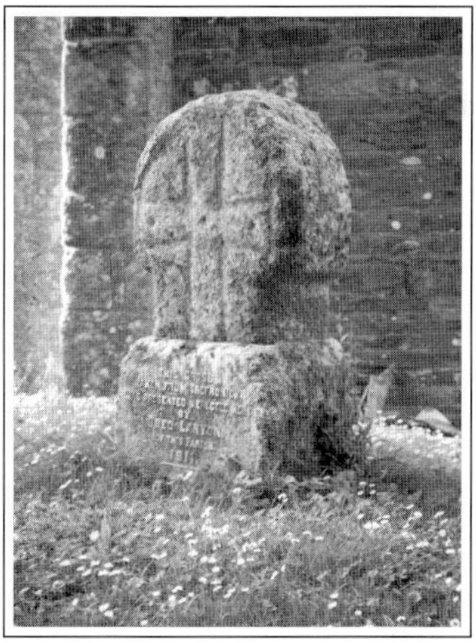

Arthur Langdon was originally informed about this massive cross-head in 1890 by Mr Thomas Clark of Truro. He stated that the stone was in use as a step at the back entrance to the farmhouse at Trefronick. Langdon, in the company of Dr William J. Stephens, a local historian from Newquay, visited Trefronick Farm in 1909 and arranged with the owner, Mr O. Lanyon, for the stone to be removed and restored. This was completed in 1911, when the monument was removed to the churchyard and set up on a modern base by Rev Buck.

A plaque fixed to the base-stone reads; *"This cross taken from Trefronick was presented and erected here by Obed Lanyon of this parish 1911"*.

The front face of the cross-head displays a cross in shallow relief with the upper and horizontal limbs slightly expanded at their ends. It appears probable that the cross was originally of latin type with the lower limb extending down the shaft. The reverse face is somewhat unusual, displaying an incised cross, emphasized by small drillings at the centre and ends of the limbs.

A replica of this cross can be seen in Kenwyn churchyard, placed as a memorial stone over the grave of the Rev Eustace Stukely Buck of Bosvigo and his wife. He was rector of St Allen for 25 years and died in 1922.

Height 2ft 6ins (0.76M) , width of head 2ft 3ins (0.685M), width of shaft 1ft 6ins (0.46M) , thickness 1ft 1ins(0.33M).

5

Trevalsa or Lower Town Cross St Allen

WHEEL-HEADED WAYSIDE CROSS

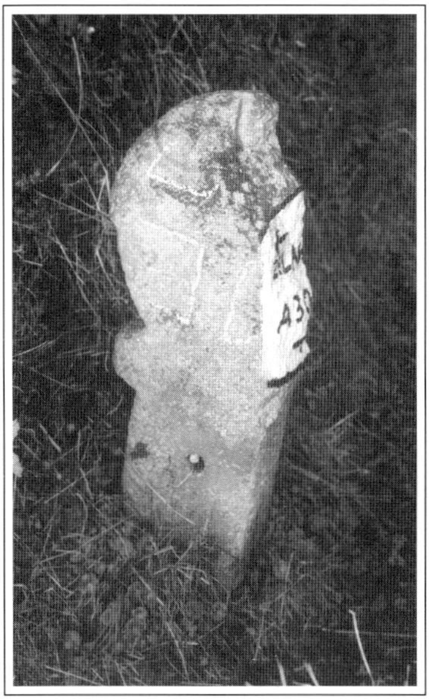

SW 8170 5183 - The cross is situated 1/3 mile east of the village of Zelah, at a road junction near Trevalsa Farm. Access - unlimited.

According to Langdon, who had been informed by Mr Thomas Clark of Truro, this cross was formerly buried head down in the ground in use as a gatepost at a field known as Twelve O'Clock Meadow, near Trevalsa. Langdon received several reports from Mr Clark about crosses that existed in St Allen parish, and recorded this cross in two separate entries: one under Trevalsa Cross and another under Lower Town Cross. In 1913, Dr William Stephens of Newquay put an end to this confusion, when be wrote his article on the St Allen Crosses for the Royal Institution of Cornwall journal. Soon after Langdon viewed the cross, it was re-erected in an old drainage ditch beside a road junction, close to its former site, where it had been used as a gatepost. During the early 1990s, the monument was regrettably disfigured by painting the side of the stone white and using it as a direction post, with the words *to Zelah* and *to the A30* being painted on it in large black letters. The author condemned this action, especially as the cross is a Scheduled Ancient Monument and therefore supposedly protected by law from damage. In August 1993 the author contacted the County Highways department about the paint damage to the cross and was later pleased to be told that they had removed it.

A third of the monument's wheel-head was broken off and lost when it was converted to use as a gatepost, but amazingly it was rediscovered in 1981 by Mr S. Reed of Trerice Farm, and placed in the church for preservation. In 1996, a project was drawn up to re-unite the loose fragment of cross to the monument and re-erect it on a new granite base-stone on the grass verge, close to its existing site. On Wednesday 15th August 1996, the cross was removed from the drainage ditch and taken for restoration by stone-work conservators Sue and Lawrence Kelland. In the meantime, with the assistance of David Attwell of the North Cornwall Heritage Coast and Countryside Service, a moorland granite boulder was purchased from St Breward to act as the new base-stone and a mortice cut in it by stonemason Ernie Hilson of St Tudy. On the 29th August, the new base-stone was installed, and on the 29th November the restored cross was returned and set up in the base-stone.

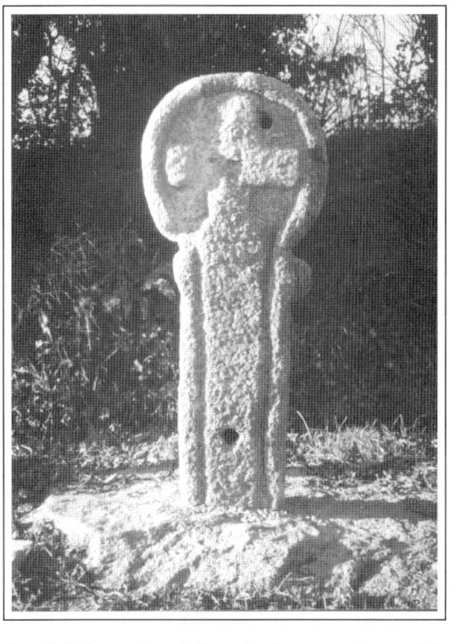

One face of the monument displays an equal-limbed cross in relief enclosed in a bead, while the reverse face shows a broad-limbed latin cross, the lower limb of which extends the full length of the shaft, merging with the deeply incised lines which form the bead or roll-moulding. The lower limb is much wider.

Height 3ft 7 1/2ins (1.1M), width of head (fractured) 12 1/2ins (0.315M), width of shaft 9 3/4ins (0.245M), width of head (originally) approx. 1ft 6ins (0.46M), thickness 8ins (0.2M).

6

Cross-head fragment
St Allen

GOTHIC LATIN CROSS

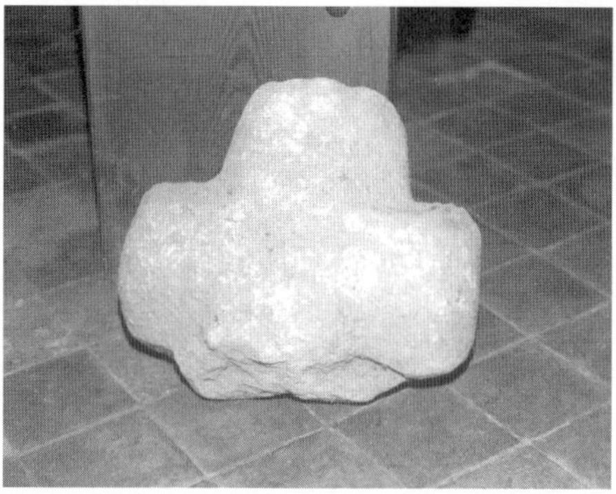

SW 8225 5060 - Inside the parish church, near the chancel. Access - When the church is unlocked, normally during daylight hours.

This small fragment of a granite latin cross consists of the upper and horizontal limbs with a short portion of octagonal sectioned shaft. It was discovered in 1862 at the same time as the Churchyard Cross no 2 (see no 3 in this guide). The fragment is now preserved in the church, lying on the floor near the chancel. The author hopes that a more appropriate and secure location for this monument can be found within the parish church.

Height 1ft (0.305M), width of shaft 8ins (0.2M) , width of limbs 7ins (0.178M), width across horizontal limbs 1ft 3ins (0.38M), thickness 7 1/2ins (0.19M).

7

Cross-base font
St Allen

GOTHIC CROSS-BASE

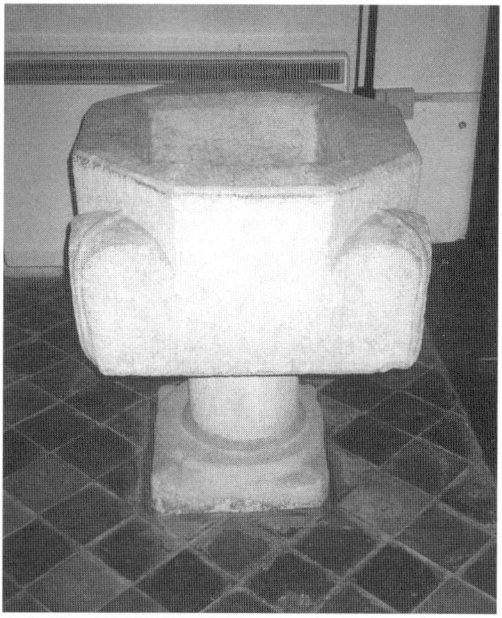

SW 8225 5060 - Inside the parish church of St. Allen. Access - When the church is unlocked, normally during daylight hours.

It is surprising to discover that the font at St Allen church has been adapted from a fine gothic cross-base, made from Pentewan stone. The cross-base is similar in design to the bases at Creed Lane, Creed and the market cross-base at Grampound (see nos 23 and 24 in this guide). Nothing is known of when the base was adapted. The cross-base has been set up on a round Pentewan stone column and base, and the socket enlarged to form the bowl of the font.

Although the author knows of several fonts that have been adapted from the shafts of ancient crosses, this is the only one where a cross-base has been re-used. In was first recorded as the remains of a cross-base by Cornish historian Charles Henderson in the 1920s.

Width of base-stone 2ft 1 1/2ins square (0.65M sq.), height 1ft 2 3/4ins (0.375M), mortice now 1ft 3 1/4ins square (0.385M), depth 7 1/4ins (0.185M).

8

Treverbyn Cross St Austell

LATIN CROSS

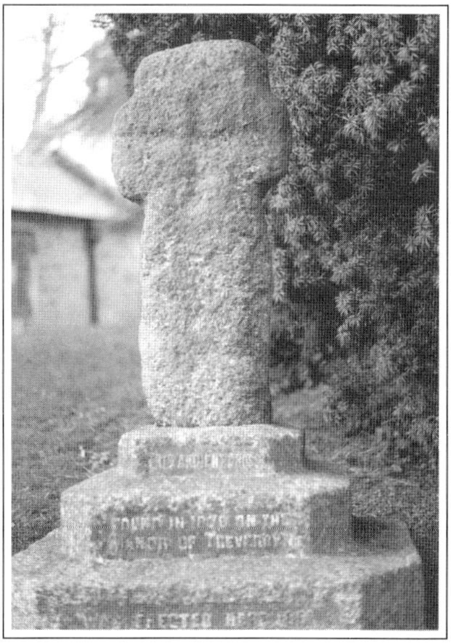

SX 0102 5135 - The cross stands on the south-eastern side of St Austell churchyard. Access - Unlimited.

This small latin cross with very short, worn limbs was discovered on Treverbyn Estate in 1879. There is, however, some conjecture as to where exactly the monument was found. According to Mr S. J.Wills, a local historian from Wendron, the stone was found near the Carn Grey rock on Carclaze Downs, the manorial boundary between Treverbyn and Tewington. On the other hand, Bodmin Antiquarian, the Rev William Iago stated that the cross was found at Treverbyn, near the parish boundary between St Austell and Luxulyan, on a direct route between the ancient chapel site at Treverbyn and the Priory of Tywardreath. This site would have been a mile north-east of the location proposed by Mr Wills.

The cross was removed to the churchyard and re-erected on a modern stepped base in 1879. The stone is cut from granite and displays an incised latin cross on one face,while on the reverse is a small incised equal-limbed cross with expanded ends.

Height 2ft 6ins (0.76M), width of shaft 10 1/2ins (0.265M), width of head 1ft 2ins (0.355M) , thickness 7 1/2ins (0.19M).

9

Moor Cottage Cross St Austell

GOTHIC LATIN CROSS

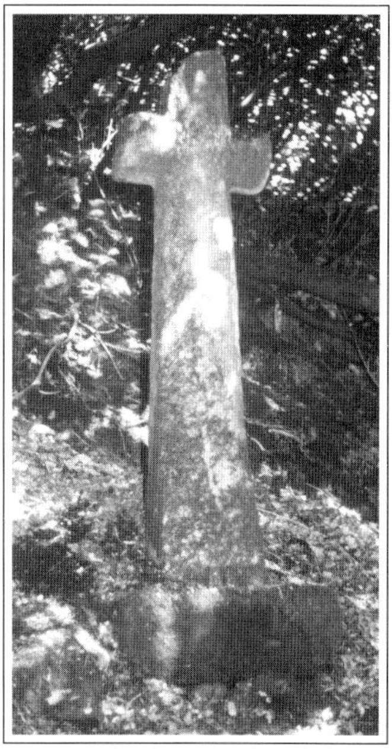

SX 0102 5135 - The cross stands in the wooded grounds of the White House on the B.3273 St Austell to Mevagissey road. Access - The monument is on private ground; there is no public access.

This complete gothic latin cross was removed to St Austell in the early 19th century. The Moor Cottage was built in 1819 and the gardens landscaped soon after, and it is probable that it was at this time that the monument was set up in the grounds. According to Henderson, the cross was brought from Hewas in the parish of Ladock. Today the cross is situated in a densely wooded area to the north of the house, now known as the White House.

The cross is octagonal in section, with pyramidal chamfer-stops at the base of the shaft. The monument is perfect except for some slight damage on the top of the upper limb. At Great Hewas there is a field known as 'Cross Park': a possible reference to its original site.

Height (including base) 7ft (2.13M), width of head 1ft 8 3/4ins (0.525M), width of shaft (at neck) 9 1/2ins (0.24M), width of shaft (at base) 1ft 2ins (0.355M), thickness 8 1/2ins to 10 3/4ins (0.215 to 0.275M), base stone, width 2ft 4ins (0.71M), height 10ins (0.255M) length unknown (partially buried).

10

Biscovey Stone
St Blazey

INSCRIBED CROSS-SHAFT

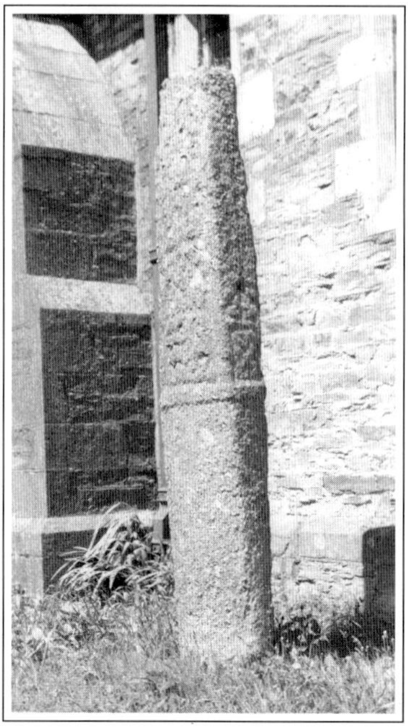

SX 0583 5359 - On the south side of the churchyard at St Mary's church, St Blazey Gate. The church is situated 2 1/2 miles north-east of St Austell on the A390. Access - Unlimited.

This inscribed cross-shaft stood for many years beside the roadside near Biscovey in use as a gatepost. In 1754, it was recorded by Borlase, who stated that many human bones had been discovered in an adjoining meadow near to where the stone was situated, suggesting that it may have been associated with a cemetery. In 1867, Polsue recorded that the stone was in use as a gatepost at St Blazey turnpike gate. It was eventually rescued in November 1896 and removed to the churchyard by the Rev D. R. Vaughan, where it remains today. The cross-head, which would have surmounted the shaft, has been lost for at least two centuries.

The decorated shaft is rectangular in section and displays an entasis, which is marked by a raised band running around the stone, dividing the shaft into two sections. The style of this cross-shaft is unusual in Cornwall, although the author has seen similar examples, with a band running around the shaft at Old Kea (see no 40 in this guide), and on monuments at Chebsey and Ilam in Staffordshire. The upper section of shaft appears to have been divided into three panels and displays interlace work, plaitwork and an inscription in Saxon lettering. The inscription has the name *Alroron* carved in three rows (Al-ro-ron) on the front of the shaft and *Ullici filius* on the back in two rows. Translated it reads: *"The stone of Alroron son of Ullici"*.

Height 7ft 10ins (2.39M), width (top) 1ft 3ins (0.38M), width (middle) 1ft ins (0.458M), thickness 6 1/2ins to 8ins (0.165M to 0.2M).

11

Latin cross in Churchyard
St Blazey

GOTHIC LATIN CROSS

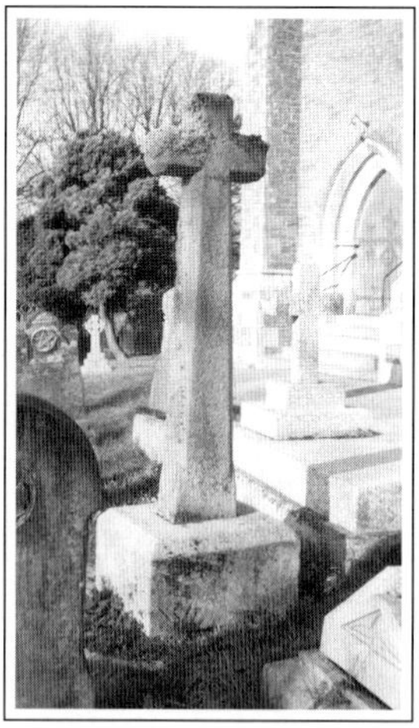

SX 0581 5357 - The monument is situated on the south side of St Mary's churchyard, StBlazey Gate. Access - Unlimited.

No history regarding this monument is known to the author. The granite cross is fractured at the neck of the stone, just below the horizontal limbs. The modern shaft has chamfered angles forming an octagonal section and tapers upwards from the modern base-stone. Below the base-stone is an old millstone. The author is doubtful about the provenance of this monument, due to its near perfect condition, but has decided to include it in this guide book, until he obtains further information.

Height 6ft 2ins (1.88M), width of shaft (at neck) 8ins (0.2M), width of shaft at (bottom) 12 1/2ins (0.305M), thickness of shaft (at neck) 7ins (0.18M), thickness of shaft (at bottom) 8ins (0.2M), width of head 1ft 9 1/2ius (0.545M).

12

Ignioc Stone
St Clement

INSCRIBED MEMORIAL CROSS

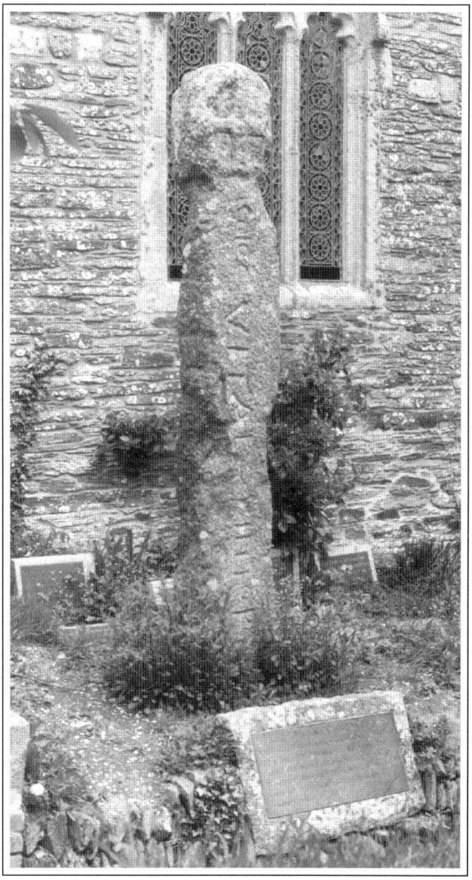

SW 8505 4387 - The stone stands on the eastern side of the south porth at St Clement churchyard. St Clement churchtown is situated 2 miles south-east of the city of Truro, beside the Tresillian river. Access - Unlimited.

This inscribed cross was first recorded in 1754 by William Borlase, in use as a gatepost close to the grounds of the vicarage at St Clement. By 1845, the Rev C. M. Gibson, the vicar of St Clement, had released the monument from this incongruous position and set it up on the drive to the vicarage garden. According to Henderson, the stone was discovered in a field on a tenement known as 'The Sanctuaries', which lies between the churchtown and the village of Malpas. The name sanctuary in this context, means simply glebe-land. The monument may have originally marked an earlier Christian burial site rather than the present churchyard. In November 1938, the stone was removed to its present postion.

The monument is of great interest. It is carved from a piece of coarse-grained granite and displays two inscriptions. The predominant and perhaps the original inscription runs vertically down the shaft and reads:- *VITALI FILI TORRICI* which translates to *VITALUS* son of *TORRICUS*. A second, and possibly later inscription in smaller characters, is a personal name IGNIOC and is displayed just below the cross-head. According to Thomas, the cross-head was carved on the stone probably in the twelth century and may have erased a portion of the second incription. It is interesting to note the re-use of this stone, which is so tall that it may have originated as a prehistoric standing stone: it has been adopted for use as a memorial stone on two separate occasions, later as a cross, and more recently as a humble gatepost. Today, an iron pin, an inch square in section, the tale-tail scars from its former use, still protudes from the face of the monument.

Some historians have suggested that the stone was originally bi-lingual, having an Ogham inscription running down the edge of the stone. Today, no Ogham script can be distinguished, and it is unclear whether, indeed, it ever existed.

A plaque below the monument reads: *The Ignioc Stone. First scheduled as a national monument 22 March 1932 when it stood in the vicarage drive from which it was removed and re-erected here 8 November 1938. Re-scheduled 12 January 1939.*

Total height (including the portion below ground) 10ft 10 1/2ins (3.315M), height above ground level 9ft 1ins (2.77M), width of head 1ft 3 1/2ins (0.395M), width of shaft 1ft 5ins to 1ft 7 1/2ins (0.43 to 0.495M), thickness 11ins to 1ft 3 1/2ins (0.28 to 0.395M).

13

Colan Cross
Colan

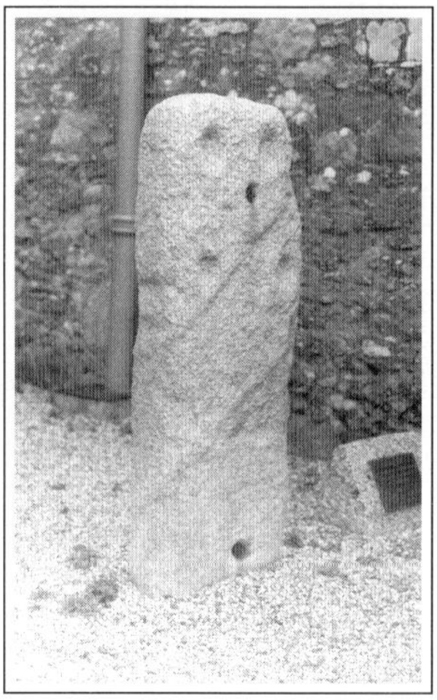

WAYSIDE CROSS-SLAB

SW 8683 6130 - The cross stands on the southern side of Colan churchyard. Colan church is situated 2 miles due east of Newquay. Access - Unlimited.

This curious looking cross-slab was discovered in 1908 by Dr W. J. Stephens, in use as a fence post beside the road leading south-east from the parish church. On finding the monument, Dr Stephens immediately contacted his friend Arthur Langdon, the Victorian authority on Cornish crosses. The cross-slab had been utilised as the last fence post and had six iron rails drilled and leaded into the back of the monument, leaving the front of the shaft unblemished except for two holes. In 1909, arrangements were made to have the monument removed from this inappropriate position and placed in the churchyard. Unfortunately these plans were dashed when the landowner refused to release the cross unless it was set up on a family grave in the churchyard. Both Stephens and Langdon would not agree to this, and so the stone remained in use as a fence post for nearly sixty more years. The project to have the cross shifted was not revived until 1970, when the Newquay Old Cornwall Society were celebrating their 50th Anniversary. The Society's President, Mr Charles Woolf, along with members and local parishioners, reached agreement with the landowner and the cross was re-erected on Friday 22nd May 1970, on the south side of the churchyard. On the following Sunday, 24th May, the ancient stone was re-dedicated by the Reverends Dennis Stafford and James Holland; finally Dr Stephens' wish had been fulfilled. The granite cross slab is crudely fashioned, with four circular depressions on the head cut to form a cross shape. The stone resembles a cross in Roche churchyard (no 80 in this guide), although different in scale and so worn that it is hard to tell whether it ever had any decoration.

Height 3ft 7 1/2ins (1.105M), width of head 1ft 3 1/2ins (0.39M), width of shaft 1ft 5 1/2ins (0.445M), thickness of shaft 6ins (0.15M).

14

Base in Churchyard
Colan

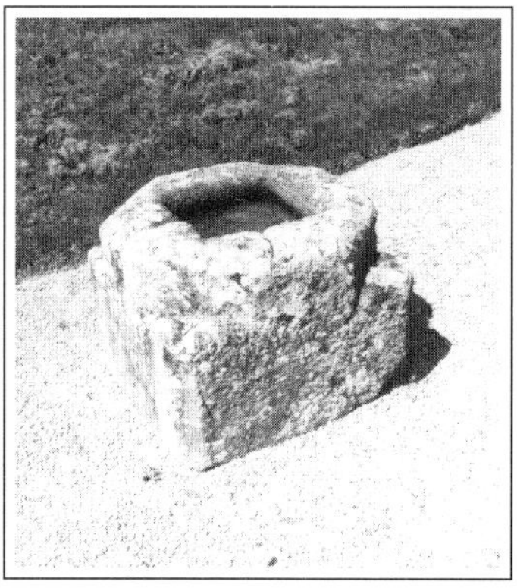

GOTHIC CROSS-BASE

SW 8681 6130 - Lies on the south-western side of Colan churchyard. Access - Unlimited.

Charles Henderson first recorded this granite base-stone, lying in the grounds of the vicarage in the 1920s. In 1971, when the vicarage was sold, the old stone was removed to the parish churchyard for preservation. The square sided base-stone has chamfered edges giving it an octagonal section and would have originally supported a medieval latin cross. Today there is no knowledge in Colan or adjoining parishes of the cross which once surmounted this massive base-stone.

Width 2ft 5ins square (0.735M), height 2ft 3ins (0.685M), mortice 1ft 1ins square (0.33M) square, mortice depth 6ins (0.15M).

15

Cross Slab
St Columb Major

INSCRIBED CROSS-SLAB

SW 9129 6366 - The stone stands on the eastern side of the south porch in St Columb Major churchyard. Access - Unlimited.

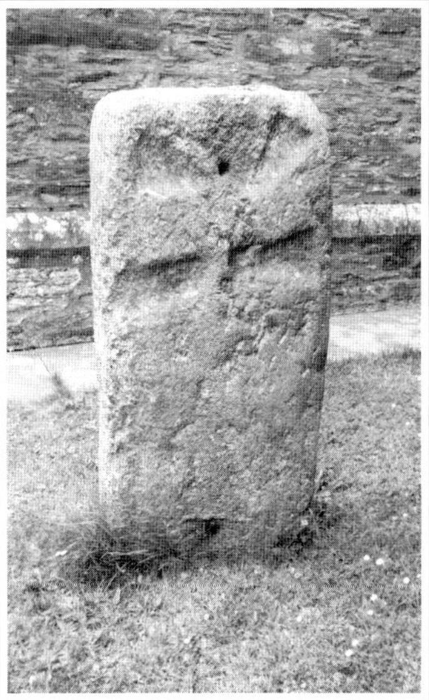

In 1858, this ancient cross-slab was recorded standing just outside the churchyard wall at St Columb Major. Prior to this it had been in use as a gatepost. The large slab of coarse-grained moorland granite has four triangular depressions cut into it on each side to form a rudely fashioned cross. According to Blight, the monument was originally inscribed, although he only identified a few characters of the inscription. The inscription was allegedly visible on the western side of the slab, but due to weathering and natural flaws in the granite, today, it is no longer visible and there is some speculation to whether it ever existed. The slab retains evidence of its former use as a gatepost, with holes where the former iron gate-hangings were inserted.

Two holes are pierced through the centre of the stone, one at ground level and another a few inches from the top of the slab. Three additional holes have been drilled in the top of the slab in the past, one of which has split a portion of the monument.

Height 4ft 5ins (1.345M), width 2ft 1ins (0.635M), thickness 10ins (0.255M).

16

Churchyard Cross-head
St Columb Major

FOUR-HOLED CHURCHYARD CROSS

SW 9132 6368 - Stands on the east side of the parish churchyard. Access - Unlimited.

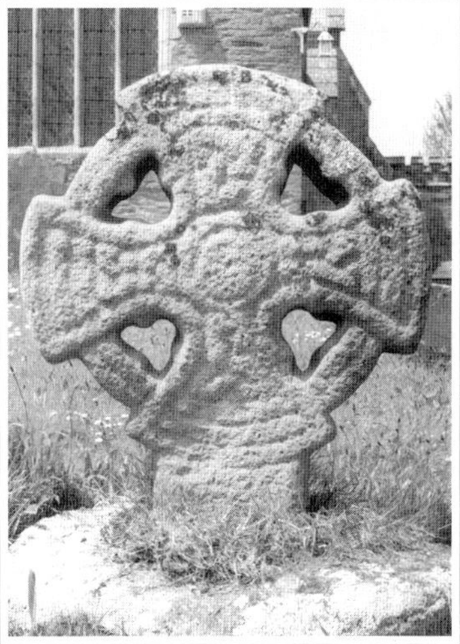

This impressive four-holed cross is cut from a piece of fine grained moorland granite. It is supported by a short section of shaft and sits in an oval shaped base-stone of similar material. Langdon suggested that due to the slender nature of the cross-shaft it may never have been any taller, although this is only speculation and without examining the bottom of the shaft it is impossible to tell. The cross-head is finely carved, with good examples of cusps formed between the outer ring and limbs of the monument. A double bead runs around the outer ring and ends of the limbs with a single bead running around the full exterior of the limbs. On the eastern side of the cross-head the monument displays a central boss and on the upper, lower and right-hand limbs triquetra knots are displayed, with a double Stafford knot on the left-hand limb. On the reverse, or western side, the monument is very worn and any decoration which existed has now been lost. It is possible that at some period in the past the cross-head lay face-down in the ground and that it became worn due to many people walking over it. The monument has been recognised as being a well proportioned cross and has been extensively copied over the years for modern Cornish memorials.

Height 3ft 1ins (0.94M), width of shaft 1ft (0.305M), base-stone diameter 3ft 2ins (0.965M), width of cross-head 2ft 9ins (0.84M), thickness of shaft 5ins (0.125M), thickness of base-stone 8ins (0.205M).

17

Black Cross
St Columb Major

LATIN WAYSIDE CROSS

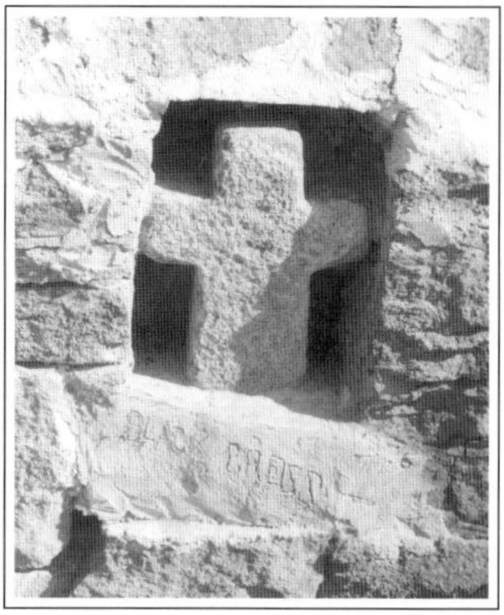

SW 9098 6066 - Built into a recess in a garden wall beside the former A39 St Columb Major to Fraddon Road. Today, the village is by-passed. Access - Unlimited.

The village of Black Cross takes its name from this small latin cross, which until the turn of the century was painted black. In more recent years it had became increasingly difficult to see, because it was built into a wall heavily shrouded in ivy. The majority of people travelling through the village could not have known that the cross existed until 1985, when a vehicle travelling towards Fraddon hit the wall, loosening the stonework. As a result, the owner of the cottage, Mr Beswetherick, had the cross repositioned in a recess in the wall and the whole wall cleared of vegetation.

Today, the stone is clear to see when passing through the village and it has recently been painted black again. No history of the monument is known. The writer suggests that the stone would have originally been taller and may have once been set up at the crossroads 100 yards to the north. On the Tithe Apportionment map of 1840, a field adjacent to the western side of the crossroads is called Cross Meadow, and may represent the original site of the Black Cross. In this position, it would have functioned as a wayside cross, guiding people from the villages of St Columb Road and Trevarren to the parish church at St Columb Major.

Height 1ft 3ins (0.38M), width of shaft 6 1/2ins (0.165M), width of head 12 1/2ins (0.315M), thickness 5 3/4ins (0.145).

18

Cross Putty
St Columb Major

GOTHIC CROSS-BASE

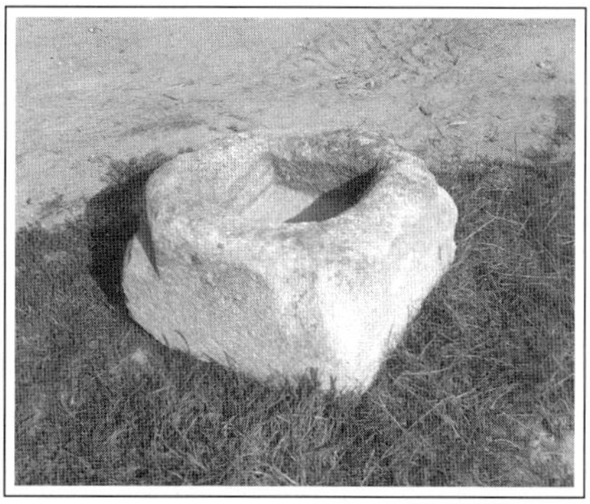

SW 9014 6308 - Beside the A3059 St Columb to Newquay road at a crossroads 1 mile west of St Columb Major town. Access - Unlimited.

When Charles Henderson first noted the existence of this base-stone in the 1920s, he considered it was probably *in situ*. According to the Tithe Apportionment map of 1840, a field on either side of the monument bears the names Cross Park and Cross Putty, indicating that although the stone may not now be *in situ* it is still close to its original site. However, later in 1951 and again in 1976, the stone was repositioned, due to road alterations at the junction. The photograph shows the cross-base in 1976, when it was removed from the ground. Today, this fine granite Gothic base-stone lies buried up to its neck in soil and has been adopted as one of the parish hurling goals. Most local people in the St Columb Major area know the stone as Cross Putty; a hurling goal, but few realise its true origins. Documentary evidence suggests that there was a market cross in the centre of St Columb in 1422; this would have been contemporary with the Cross Putty; but no remains are now known.

There is also a site marked on a town plan of 1856 called the Fish Cross, situated near the Market Place, which probably referred to the same monument.

Width 2ft 4ins (0.71M) x 2ft 3ins (0.685M), height 1ft 4ins (0.405M), mortice 1ft 2ins (0.355) x 1ft 2 1/2ins (0.37M), depth of mortice 7 1/2ins (0.19M).

19

Tregonetha Downs Base St Columb Major

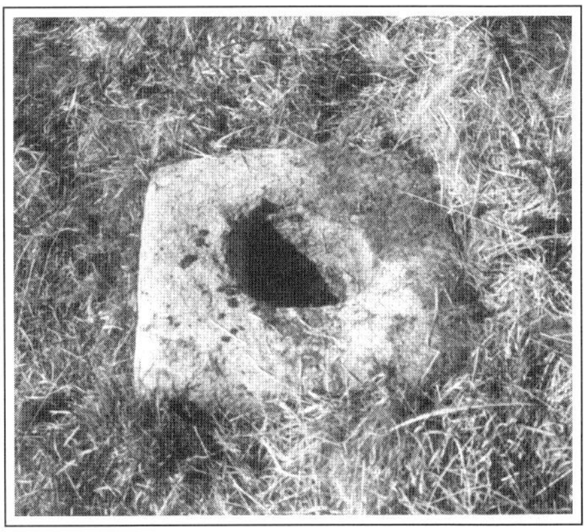

CROSS-BASE OF BOUNDARY CROSS

SW 9567 6266 - Within a few feet of the parish boundary on Tregonetha Downs. Access - Tregonetha Downs is privately owned; the author has been unable to ascertain whether there is any public access.

This small cross-base stands approximately one hundred metres north-west of the 'Crossy Ann' boundary cross (see no 97 in this guide). The author has no information about the monument which formerly stood in the socket, which like Crossy Ann must have originally marked the parish boundary between St Columb Major and St Wenn. Today the old stone has been moved a few feet into St Columb parish and lies half hidden in bracken on the Downs. The granite cross-base is almost square in section with a square mortice and appears to be of Gothic date and much later than the nearby 'Crossy Ann' stone.

Width 1ft 10 3/4ins (0.58M) by 1ft 11 1/4ins (0.595M), mortice 11ins (0.28M) by 10ins (0.255M), depth 7 1/2ins (0.19M).

20

Doublestiles Cross St Columb Minor

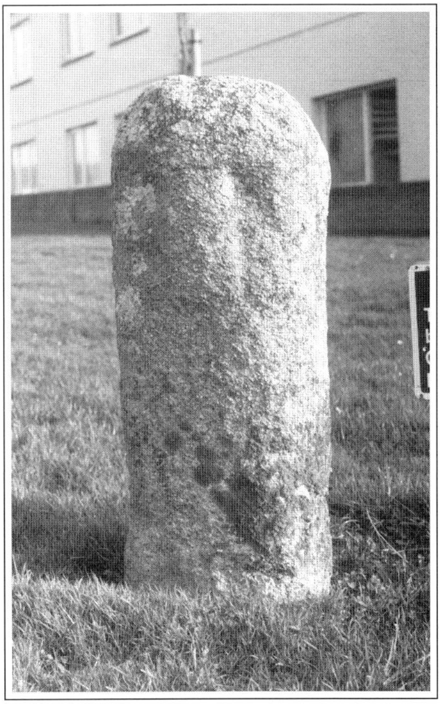

CROSS PILLAR

SW 8344 6202 - On a grass verge at a junction between Henver Road and Duchy Avenue, which leads to Cross Close. Access - Unlimited.

This rude cross pillar or slab originally stood in a field known as Cross Close and was moved to its present position when the adjacent housing estate was built in 1954, although the monument is still close to its former position. The stone is unusual, being a granite pillar of oval section. The southern face displays the remains of an expanded-limbed cross in relief of irregular length limbs. The top of the pillar appears to have originally been taller, as only a fragment of the cross symbol's upper limb can now be discerned. Blight stated that a cross of similar style existed on the reverse face, although the marking here is now is faint and worn.

The cross is known as Double Stiles or Three Stiles Cross, probably due to the stiles on the church path which lead through the field of Cross Close.

Height 3ft 1ins (0.94M), thickness 11 1/2ins (0.293M), width of shaft 1ft 2 1/2ins (0.37M).

21

Treloy Hill Cross, St Columb Minor

GOTHIC CROSS-SHAFT

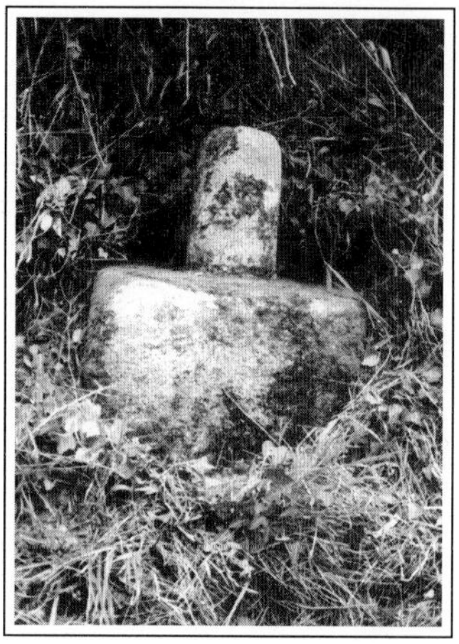

SW 8543 6241 - Beside the A3059 Newquay to St Columb Major road, 1/2 mile east of Rialton Manor on Treloy Hill, locally known as Treskeys Hill. Access - Unlimited.

In 1858, Blight recorded that a cross stood by the roadside between Higher and Lower St Columb, but did not state whether the monument was complete or what style of cross it was. Later in 1884, Oliver noted an interesting fact that the Gothic cross-base was inscribed with the letters T. S. In the author's opinion these initials were probably those of a landowner, and at some point in history the stone may have been re-used as a private boundary stone (see no 45 in this guide). There is some conjecture as to whether the monument was shifted to St Columb Minor churchtown in the 1920s. Today it sits high up on a grass bank on a sharp left-hand bend. Visitors should take extreme caution when visiting the stone as traffic passes close to the grass bank.

Early in 1992, while travelling along the A3059, the author was surprised to notice that the octagonal cross-shaft was missing. On closer examination the shaft was found to have been snapped off, leaving a fragment still cemented in the base-stone. Later, a search of the area resulted in the shaft being found discarded in the hedge on the opposite side of the road. In July 1992, after consultation with members of Newquay Old Cornwall Society, the author, along with Mr H. Barriball, had the two portions of monument reunited with the aid of a stainless steel pin and mortar.

Height of shaft 1ft 3ins (0.38M), width of shaft 7 1/2ins (0.19M), base-stone 1ft 11ins square (0.585M), height 1ft 4ins (0.405M).

22

Lavethan Cross, St Columb Minor

LATIN WAYSIDE CROSS

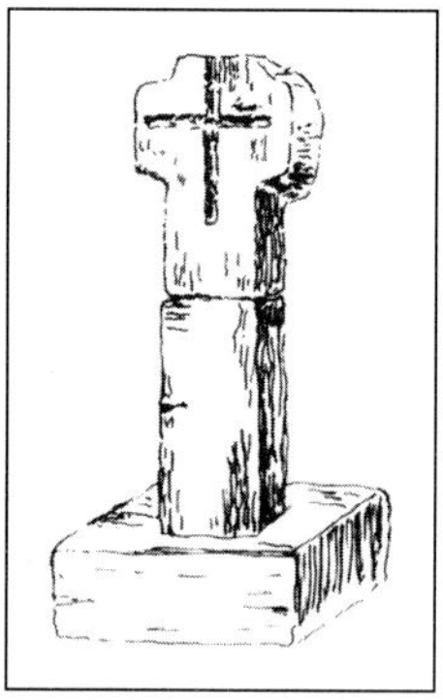

Stands in the garden of a cottage at Mount Wise, Newquay. Access - There is no public access.

According to Blight this cross was removed from Blisland Moor and placed in the grounds of Lavethan Manor at Blisland for preservation, along with three other crosses. At the beginning of the century the monument was removed from Lavethan and re-erected in the grounds of Tregaddick House, a property 1/2 mile north-east of the latter. Both properties were owned by the Morshead family, and at Tregaddick another two crosses had been erected, 'rescued' from the moor. Here in 1985, the author viewed these stones together with two 'mock' crosses: the bases of cheese presses set up on granite shafts. Early in 1991, the crosses were sold and removed to new sites. One was taken to Newquay and another to St Just (see West Penwith no 37).

This latin cross has been considerably damaged over the centuries and only a few inches of its square sectioned limbs have survived. It is the opinion of the author that the sale of Cornwall's monuments is an outrage which should not be allowed. These crosses were originally the property of the parish and were never intended to be the private property of an individual. The only consolation in this particular case is that the cross was not removed out of the county.

Height 2ft 3ins (0.685), width of shaft 9ins (0.23M), width of head 1ft 2ins (0.355M), thickness 8 1/2ins (0.215M).

23

Creed Lane Cross-base, Creed with Grampound

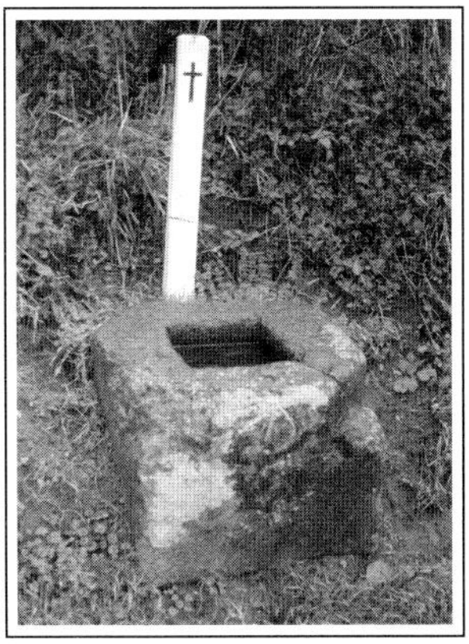

GOTHIC BASE-STONE

SW 9350 4787 - Situated on a minor road which leads from the village of Grampound, south to Creed church. Access - Unlimited.

A clause in the Will of Dr Reginald Mertherderwa, Principal of Bull Hall, Oxford, and Rector of Creed church from 1423 to 1447, dated February 11th 1447 read: *'New stone crosses to be put up of the usual kind in those parts of Cornwall from Kayar Reslasek to Camborne church where dead bodies are rested on the way to their burial, that prayers may be made and the bearers take some rest'.* There are no Gothic crosses in Camborne parish or any of the surrounding parishes, and it has been suggested that these crosses were set up in Creed instead. In the parish of Creed with Grampound, where the doctor was rector, there are the remains of four crosses of 15th century date, three of which are cut from Pentewan stone.

At Creed Lane, on the way to the parish church, is a large cross-base on the left-hand side of the road, which is said to be *in situ*. The base-stone is similar in style to the one supporting the Market Cross in Grampound village. The stone is octagonal in section and, although complete, it has been defaced by the addition of an Ordnance Survey bench mark.

Base-stone 1ft 11ins square (0.585M square), height 1ft 5 1/2 ins (0.445M), mortice 10ins square (0.255M square), mortice depth 4 1/2ins (0.115M).

24

Market Cross Creed with Grampound

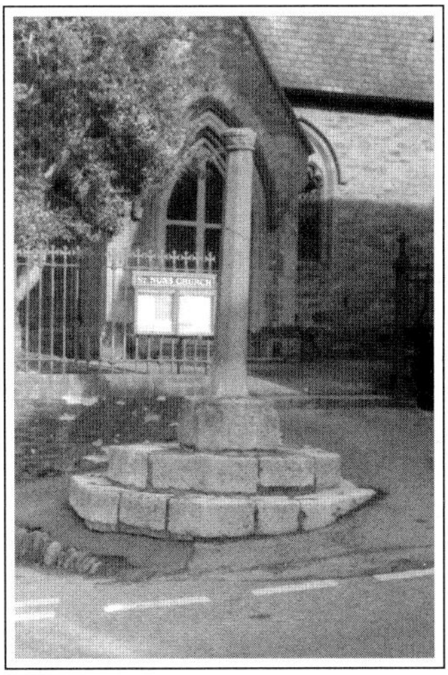

GOTHIC LATIN or LANTERN CROSS

SW 9360 4828 - Situated beside St Naunter's or St Nuns Chapel in the centre of Grampound. Access - Unlimited.

This fine market cross of Pentewan stone stands *in situ* at the centre of the historic town of Grampound, between St Nuns chapel and the A390 road. The monument was well illustrated by Blight in 1858, who showed a fracture on the shaft and its cross-head missing. Since this time the stone has suffered no noticeable deterioration. The cross is of 15th century date and is more ornate than the three other crosses in the parish of Creed with Grampound.

The tapered shaft is octagonal in section and displays chamfer-stops at its base. A fracture can still be seen two feet from the top. Originally, the shaft would have been surmounted by either a latin or lantern cross-head. An unusual feature of this monument is the decorative collar at the top of the cross shaft; which was worked from a separate piece of stone and fitted between the cross-head and shaft. The large Gothic base-stone which supports the cross-shaft has been fractured in the past, but is still complete and is in turn supported by a stepped-base made from large blocks of Pentewan stone clamped together with ironwork. This site would have been a hive of activity on market days with traders congregating around the cross. Today travellers rush through the village by car, and most never notice this splendid monument.

Total height (excluding stepped base) 8ft 2ins (2.49M), width of shaft (neck) 8 1/2ins (0.215M), width of shaft (at base) 1ft 1/2ins (0.32M), base stone 2ft 5 1/2ins (0.75M), base stone height 1ft 6ins (0.46M).

Fair Cross
Creed with Grampound

GOTHIC LATIN BOUNDARY CROSS

SW 9556 4735 - Close to the junction of the B3287 Tregony to St Austell road and a minor road to Grampound. Access - Unlimited.

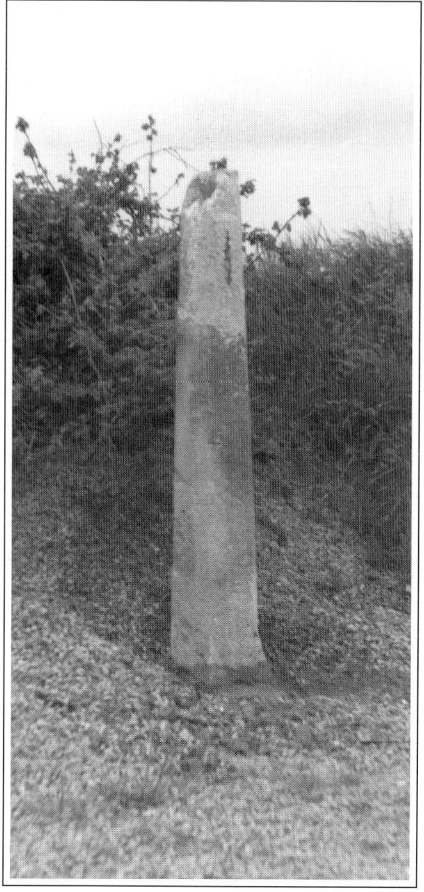

This Gothic cross-shaft of Pentewan stone stands fifty metres east of the road junction known as Fair Cross. At this road junction lies the parish boundary between Creed with Grampound and Cuby and the author suggests that the cross may have originally marked this boundary. According to the Tithe Apportionment map of 1840, the field directly behind the cross is known as Cross Close, while the fields directly opposite are known as Yonder Fair Cross and Little Fair Cross. These field names provide some evidence that the cross, although not *in situ*, is close to its original site. The cross-shaft is octagonal in section and tapers from the ground upwards. The top of the cross-shaft has a six-inch hole drilled in it, which formerly held a dowel to receive the cross-head. The eastern face of the shaft has been cut away at the top exposing the hole. During the last thirty years the ground level has been raised considerably, due to road alterations. When Mary Henderson recorded the shaft in 1973, it measured 6 feet 4 inches and displayed pyramidal chamfer-stops at the base of the shaft. The photograph shown here was taken at this time. According to Charles Henderson, the shaft stands in the fractured remains of half the original base-stone. Today, the cross-shaft is only four feet above the present ground level, and both the chamfer-stops and the base-stone are no longer visible. The monument is scarred by graffiti and also an Ordnance Survey bench-mark, the latter being now below ground level. The graffiti consists of three sets of initals and a date, carved on the southern faces of the shaft: R D, C J, 1920 and LM. The author originally only found two sets of initals and suggested that the cross-shaft may have been adopted as a private bound stone, with the initals being that of the landowners. Since he has found a third set of initals he concludes that it is graffiti, probably carved by local boys.

During the early 1990s, the County Council started white-washing the cross-shaft along with other bound stones and mileposts in the locality. This the author has objected to, as it has ruined the appearance of this buff-coloured local Pentewan stone. In recent years the practise of whitewashing the stone has been ceased and the paint is slowly flaking off, although it may take several more years.

The author considers it unfortunate that the ground level has been raised so much, concealing both the chamfered-stops and any chance of examining the alleged cross-base.

Height above ground level 4ft (1.22M), width of shaft (at top) 7 1/2ins (0.19M), width of shaft (at ground level) 9 1/2ins (0.24M), width across flats (at top) 3 1/2ins (0.09 M), width across flats (at ground level) 4 1/2ins (0.115M).

Nancor Cross
Creed with Grampound

GOTHIC LATIN CROSS

SW 9446 4840 - Situated high up on an embankment beside the A390 Truro to St Austell road at the top of Grampound Hill. Access - Unlimited.

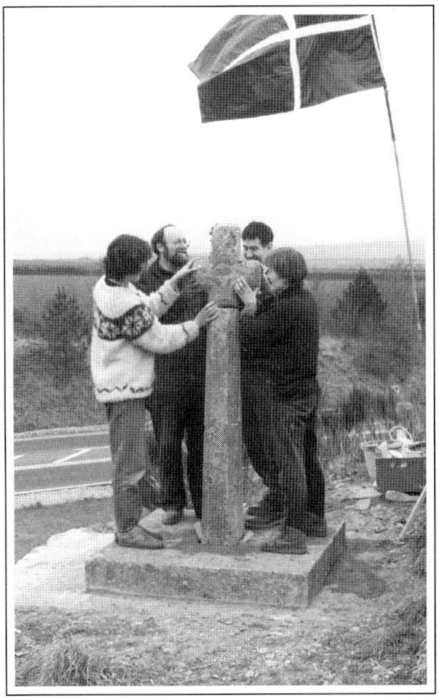

This cross-head of fine grained granite was discovered during the 1920s by Arthur Mannell who was the local lengthsman (clearer of ditches) for the County Council. The road was widened between Nancor Farm and Carwinnick Lane, and the cross-head was found buried in the hedge when it was removed. The latin cross-head, which is octagonal in section, has a curious Crucifix figure carved in relief upon it. Christ is depicted exhibiting an unusual headdress, with arms outstretched and slightly raised. Later, the cross-head was mounted on a new octagonal-sectioned granite shaft and stepped-base carved to suitable proportions and funded by J. C. Williams Esq. of Caerhays Castle. The completed monument was set up at the junction of the A390 road with a minor road to Nancor and Carwinnick, close to where it was discovered. Here the monument stood for many years despite having its cross-head broken off and repaired on several occasions. In 1984 the monument was removed when major road improvements commenced on the A390 and was later re-erected on a grass verge beside a newly formed junction. There are two fields mentioned on the Tithe Apportionment Map of 1840 under Nancor, ' Cross Close' which is close to the road junction and 'Cross Close Meadow', which is at Nancor Farm: both could be connected with the cross. Some local people have tried to make a connection between the head of Nancor Cross and the shaft of Fair Cross (see no 25 in this guide), which has lost its head, but the author does not believe that they are related, both have 'cross' field names close to their sites and the monuments are cut from different materials, Nancor Cross is cut from granite and Fair Cross from Pentewan Stone.

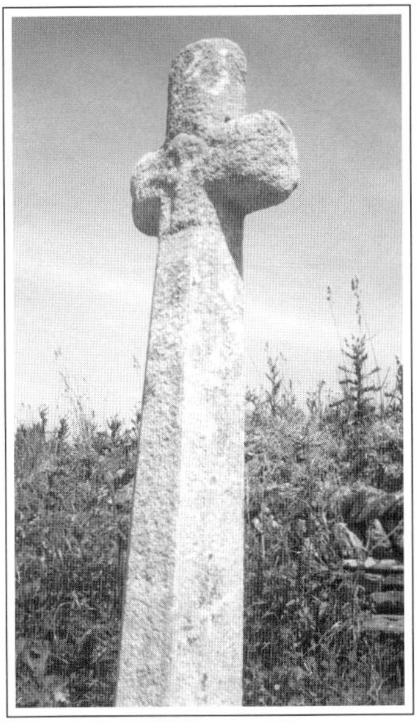

On the 1st Februrary 1995, the cross was discovered smashed into four pieces and lying by the roadside. The cross appeared to have been deliberately vandalised, the cross-head had been hit with an heavy object, pushing it backwards. The modern shaft hit the top step of the cross-base, fracturing the shaft mid-way. The lower part of the cross-head was split off at the point at which the head had been attached to the shaft. In 1996, a project was arranged to restore and re-position the cross on the adjacent side of the road junction, high up on the embankment. A new platform was created by the Council Council under the supervision of Mr Dave Stark. On St Piran's Day 1996, the cross was repaired by Sue and Lawrence Kelland, assisted by the author and Ann Preston-Jones of English Heritage. The fractures in the monument were pinned together with the aid of phosphor-bronze dowels and fixed in position with polyester stone mastic. The joints were then filled with a lime-based mortar, coloured to match the stone.

Total height 7ft (2.135M), width of head 1ft 3ins (0.38M), height of head 1ft 5 1/2ins (0.445M), thickness 6 1/2ins (0.165M)

27

Ellenglaze Cross
Cubert

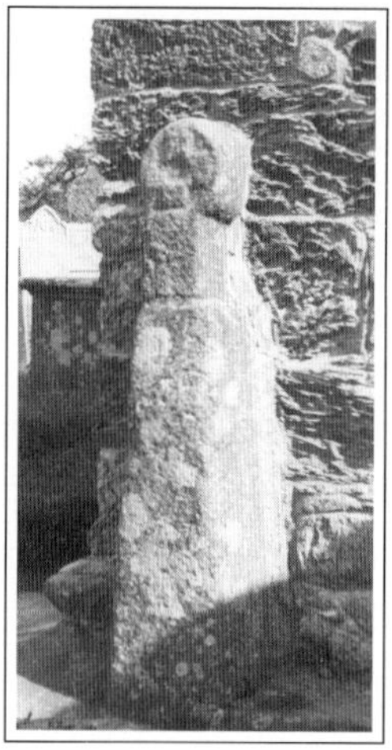

WHEEL-HEADED BOUNDARY or WAYSIDE CROSS

SW 7862 5776 - The cross is situated on the N.W. side of Cubert churchyard. Cubert is 5 miles S.W. of Newquay. Access - Unlimited.

In 1860, this small cross was removed from Ellenglaze Lane and brought into the churchyard for preservation. Here it was set up against the western side of the north transept on a tall granite shaft. The two stones are not related, although some historians believe the shaft may itself be ancient. Elllenglaze is a farm lying in a valley 1 mile south-west of the churchtown and is situated on the boundary between the parishes of Cubert and Perranzabuloe. The cross-head displays an equal-limbed cross in relief, with wide limbs, it is enclosed in a narrow bead and has a square depression centrally positioned between the limbs instead of a boss. The reverse face is inaccessible in its present position.

Height 1ft 10ins (0.56M), width of head 1ft 1/2ins (0.32M), width of shaft 8 1/2ins (0.215M), thickness 6 1/2ins (0.165M).

28

Churchyard Cross
St Dennis

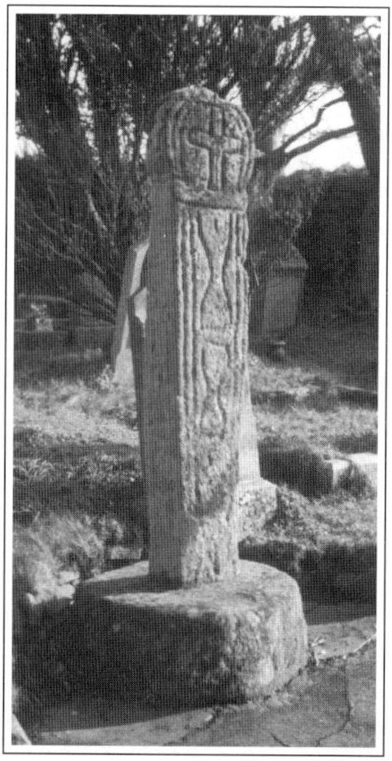

WHEEL-HEADED CHURCHYARD CROSS

SW 9507 5828 - Stands on the south side of St Dennis parish churchyard, St Dennis is situated 7 miles N.W. of St Austell. Access - Unlimited.

This fine incised granite cross stands *in situ* in the churchyard, which is on the site of an Iron Age hillfort. The monument has several unusual features, first of which is that the cross-head is almost horseshoe-shaped, similar to the Mexico Cross at Phillack (see West Cornwall no 81). On the head, on both faces, is an incised latin cross, the reverse face having rounded ends to the limbs and two round depressions below the horizontal limbs. The head has a double bead extending around it which meets a wide collar at the neck. The shaft is at its widest at the neck of the monument and tapers downwards to its round base-stone. The front of the shaft also has a double bead running down from the collar to the base-stone and is decorated with three incised symbols, similar in shape to one that adorns the Nine Maidens Down Cross at Clowance in the parish of Crowan (see West Cornwall no 31). These symbols may represent an hour glass or Holy chalice. Alternatively, Dexter suggested that they were pagan symbols representing double-headed axes. The reverse face of the shaft also has one of these curious symbols with yet more incised panels on the sides of the shaft.

Height 6ft 7ins (2.007M), width of shaft (at neck) 1ft 3 1/2ins (0.395M), width of head 1ft 6ins (0.46M), width of shaft (at base) 1ft (0.305M), thickness (at neck) 8 1/2ins (0.215M), thickness (at base) 7ins (0.18M), base-stone diameter 2ft 11ins (0.89M), base height 1ft 2ins (0.355M).

29

Fraddon Cross
St Enoder with Mitchell

WHEEL-HEADED CROSS

SW 8924 5694 - Stands on the south side of St Enoder churchyard. St Enoder is 6 miles south-west of St Columb Major. Access - Unlimited.

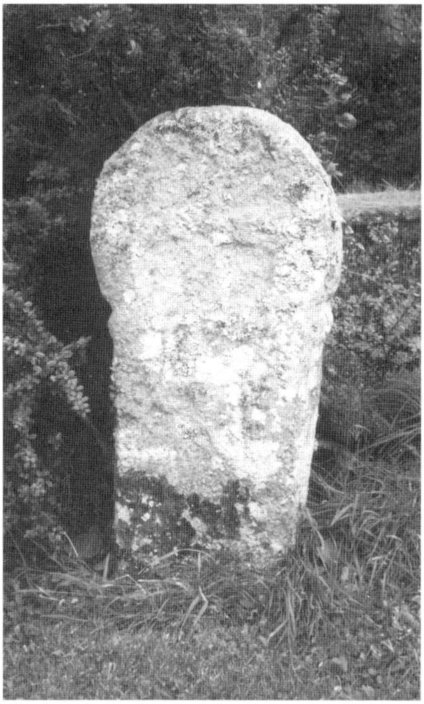

This cross was discovered buried head down in the ground beside the road from St Enoder to the village of Fraddon. The cross was removed to the churchyard by Mr Charles Bice in April 1879 and placed on the north side. Here it remained until 1893 when it was repositioned by the Rev L. Horsburgh in its present site on the left-hand side of the lych gate on the south side of the churchyard.

The front of this monument displays an equal-limbed cross formed by cutting four triangular depressions, bringing the cross into relief. On the reverse face is an unusual sunken cross cut into the stone, its execution being somewhat more crude than the front face. At the neck of the monument are two small projections, a feature which is seen on crosses in both North and Mid Cornwall.

On the north-east side of St Enoder churchyard can be seen the grave of Mr Charles Bice and his wife Amy, with an appropriate memorial consisting of three wheel-headed crosses, one large with a small cross on either side. The style of these crosses is similar to the Fraddon Cross, a permanent reminder of its removal into the churchyard.

Height 3ft 3 1/2ins (1M), width of head 1ft 7 1/2ins (0.495M), width of shaft (at neck) 1ft 4ins (0.405M), width of shaft (at ground level) 1ft 2ins (0.355M), thickness 7ins (0.18M).

30

South Porch Cross-base
St Enoder with Mitchell

CROSS-BASE

SW 8924 5695 - Built into the interior wall of the south porch of St Enoder parish church. Access - Only when the church is unlocked.

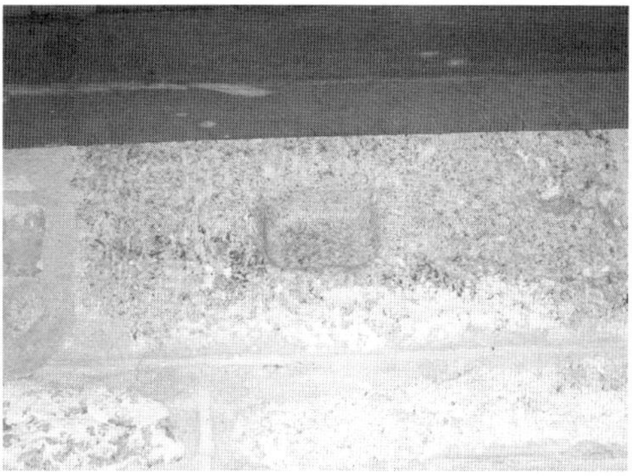

This granite base-stone of a wayside cross can be seen set into the western wall of the south porch of the parish church, high up against the roof timbers. Polsue recorded seeing a base-stone standing near the Fraddon cross in 1867. He recorded, '*By the side of the high road leading from the Church-town to Fraddon, and near the former place, is a wayside cross, its head fixed in the ground, and its basement standing on its edge by the side of it.*' The author suggests that this stone may have been retrieved at the same time as the cross, and utilised as a simple building stone during restoration work on the church in 1870.

Length 2ft 3ins (0.685M), width 1ft 6ins (0.46M), mortice 6ins by 4ins (0.15M by 0.1M), mortice depth 3ins (0.075M).

31

Beacon or Corran Cross
St Ewe

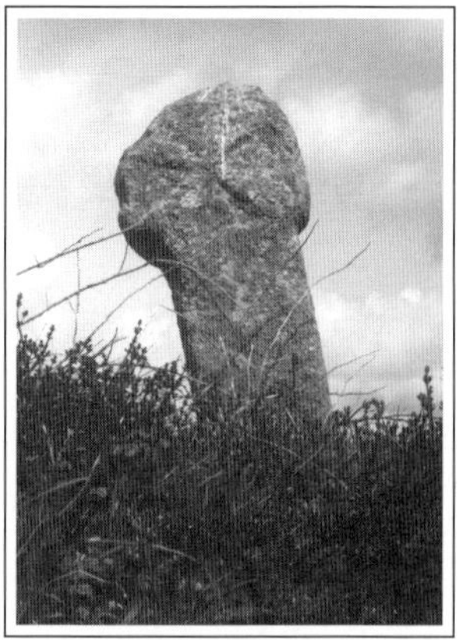

WHEEL-HEADED WAYSIDE CROSS

SW 9849 4570 - At a road junction leading from St Ewe to Gorran, 1/2 mile south-east of St Ewe churchtown. Access - Unlimited.

Visitors approach the Beacon or Corran Cross along a minor road from the top of Mevagissey, past the entrance to Heligan, following a concrete-block wall which has replaced many of the hedgerows in this area. The cross will be seen sitting on top of a hedge above a small layby after approaching a left-hand bend. This site is one of the highest points in the parish and is known as the Beacon, hence Beacon Cross; the name Corran Cross, recorded by some historians, is after the nearest farm which is half a mile north-east of the monument. The cross is near its original position marking the church path from Kestle to the churchtown, and is close to a stile leading into the field. The cross was removed prior to 1937 from this position in the hedge, in the process of creating a new lay-by. The Rural District Council had the monument re-erected on a modern base and set up on the adjoining hedge at this time.
The monument displays an equal-limbed cross on each face, formed by four triangular depressions cut into the granite. The cross-head has received a great deal of damage over the centuries and is badly chipped.

Height 3ft 5ins (1.04M), width of shaft (at neck) 1ft (0.305M), width of head 1ft 6ins (0.456M), width of shaft (at base) 1ft 2ins (0.355M), thickness 7 1/2ins (0.19M).

32

Bokiddick Cross, Heligan
St Ewe

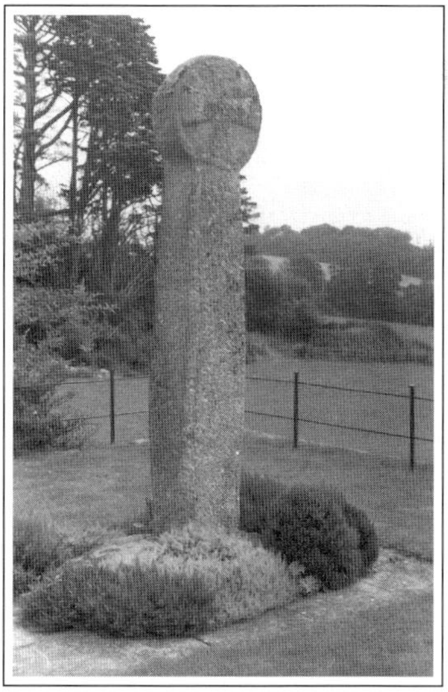

WHEEL-HEADED WAYSIDE CROSS

SW 9991 4646 - In the grounds of Heligan Manor, which is 2 miles west of the fishing port of Mevagissey. Access - The cross stands on private grounds; there is no public access.

This tall cross, which has stood close to the manor house of Heligan, the home of the Tremayne family, since the 1900s, came originally from the parish of Lanivet. It was found at Bokiddick Farm in Lanivet by a former tenant, Mr Phillips, who stated that the cross was discovered in use as a doorpost to a porch at the farmhouse. The stone had been buried head down in the ground and was retrieved from this position in 1878. At this time, Bokiddick and Heligan were both owned by the Tremayne family and this is how the ancient stone came to be removed to Heligan. Although somewhat taller than the majority of Lanivet's wayside crosses, the cross-head is of typical Lanivet style. The stone displays an equal-limbed cross in relief with expanded ends and is enclosed by a bead which runs around the head and down both sides of the shaft. Both faces are similar. The shaft, which displays fixing-holes, a sign of its former use as a doorpost, has a marked entasis. A field to the north of Bokiddick, recorded on the Tithe Apportionment map of 1839 as 'Cross Park', may indicate the original site of the monument.

Height 8ft 3ins (2.515M), width of shaft 1ft 5ins (0.43M), width of head 2ft (0.61M), thickness 11 1/4ins (0.285M).

33

Churchtown Cross
St Ewe

GOTHIC MARKET CROSS

SW 9780 4607 - Situated in the centre of St Ewe churchtown, south of the parish church. Access - Unlimited.

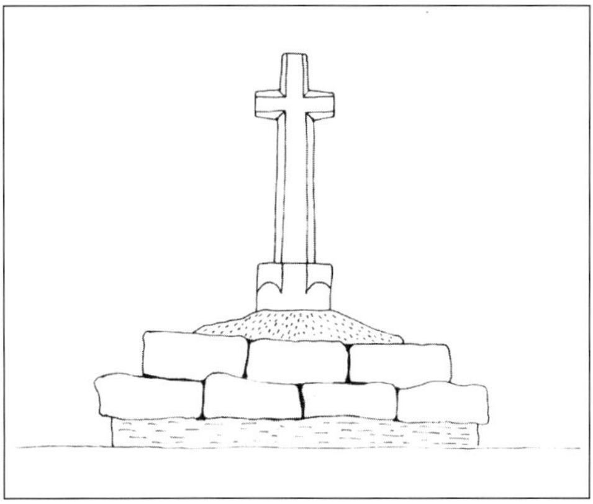

This large Gothic market cross once formed the focal point in the life of the village. It stands at the centre of St Ewe churchtown and consists of three parts, each with a different story. Today, the only original part of the monument is the massive stepped base with its cobbled platform made up from blocks of Pentewan stone and granite. Both the square shaft and its base-stone are not original and until 1866 this shaft was used to support a sundial. In 1897, Hammond, when recording the Moor Cottage Cross at St Austell (see no 9 in this guide), stated that a similar cross once stood in the churchtown at St Ewe. Further support for this was provided by Miss Johnson, the former owner of Trewithen House, who in 1920 rescued a Gothic cross-base, which had been used to wash beer bottles at the Crown Inn, almost opposite the cross-site. This base-stone was removed to Trewithen House in the parish of Probus, where it still exists (see p78 in this guide). The illustration above shows the author's suggestion of how the original monument would have looked. No knowledge of the original cross-shaft exists.

The stepped base-stone is set four square to the points of the compass and has been used for various activities over the years. The village stocks, which now stand in the church porch, were once chained to the platform and during the St Ewe fairs, which were held in April and October, the monument was used as an auctioneer's rostrum. On the western side against the base-stone is a set of steps, known as an epping block, used for mounting horses.

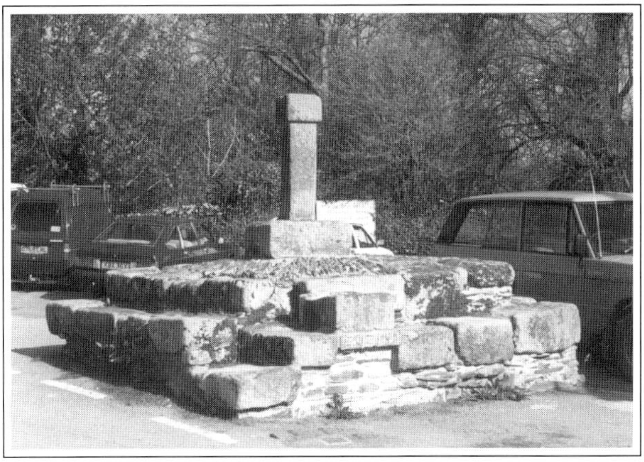

During the 1960s, St Austell Old Cornwall Society carried out repairs to this monument.

Height of shaft 3ft 8 1/2ins (1.13M), width of shaft 11 1/2ins (0.29M), thickness of shaft 10ins (0.255M), base stone 2ft 7ins square (0.788M), base stone, height 1ft 1ins (0.33M).

34

Lanhadron Cross-base
St Ewe

INSCRIBED CROSS-BASE

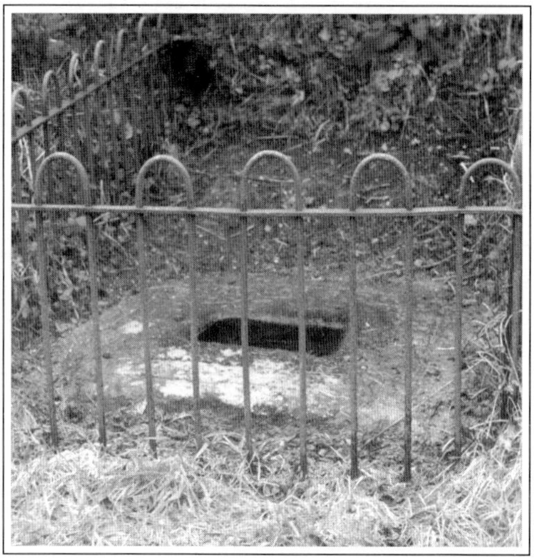

SW 9894 4783 - Stands on Nunnery Hill between the village of Polgooth and St Ewe churchtown. Access - Unlimited.

This unique monument is the only example of a pre-Norman inscribed cross-base in the county. There are several base-stones in Cornwall, which have been adopted as bound stones and have the initials of landowners inscribed on them, but none are considered ancient. The monument is recorded on the parish Tithe map of 1839. In 1873 Mr Thomas Stephens, a local parishioner, stated that funeral processions would stop at the cross and that the corpse would be carried around the monument before the bearers took a rest. Tradition suggests that a farmer in the neighbourhood unearthed the cross and base-stone, having been told that money, or treasure was buried beneath it. The cross itself has been missing since this time, although an illustration on an 18th century manuscript in the British Library, suggests that the cross-shaft was also inscribed. A copy of this was published by Elisabeth Okasha in her Corpus of *Early Christian Inscribed Stones of South-west Britain.*

The cross-base is inscribed on all four sides within an incised border enclosing the characters. Several historians have transcribed the worn Latin inscription, resulting in several different translations. The most probable opinion of the reading is *LURATECUS FECIT CRUCEM + O PRO ANIMA SUA*, which translated reads, 'LURATECUS erected this cross for the good of his soul'. The lettering has been cut in three inch characters within a six inch border on the upper face of the stone.

4ft 1ins by 3ft 10in (1.245M by 1.17M), thickness 1ft 7ins (0.48M), mortice 1ft 5ins by 1ins (0.43M by 0.305M), depth 9ins (0.23M).

35

In Feock Churchyard
Feock

GOTHIC WHEEL-HEADED CROSS

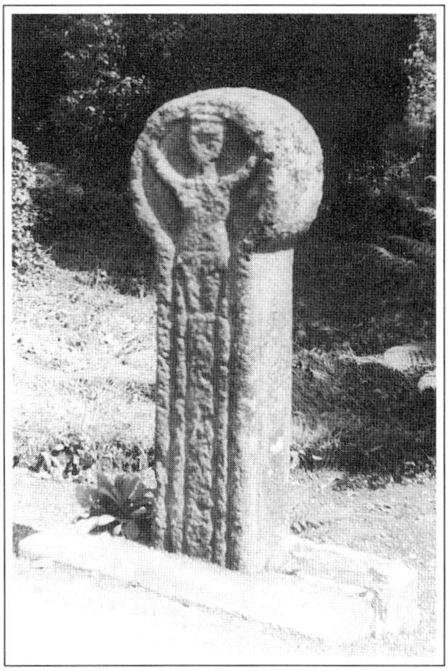

SW 8251 3841 - The cross is situated on the south side of Feock churchyard. Feock is situated 4 1/2 miles south of Truro.

This superbly crafted monument is cut from a piece of fine grey elvan. On the principle face of the head is a figure of the crowned Christ with arms outstretched within a narrow bead, which is of a 12th to early 13th century form. The legs of the figure appear to end at the knees, and the shaft has a double bead on either side of the knees which extends down to the base-stone. The reverse face shows a foliated cross of a design unique in Cornwall, but seen elsewhere on cross-slabs of 13th century date. A narrow bead or lower limb extends down the shaft from the cross with a bead running around the cross-head and down each side of the shaft.

Height 4ft (1.22M), width of head 1ft 5 1/2ins (0.445M), width of shaft 11 1/2ins (0.29M), thickness 9 1/2ins (0.24M).

36

Trelissick Garden
Feock

WHEEL-HEADED WAYSIDE CROSS

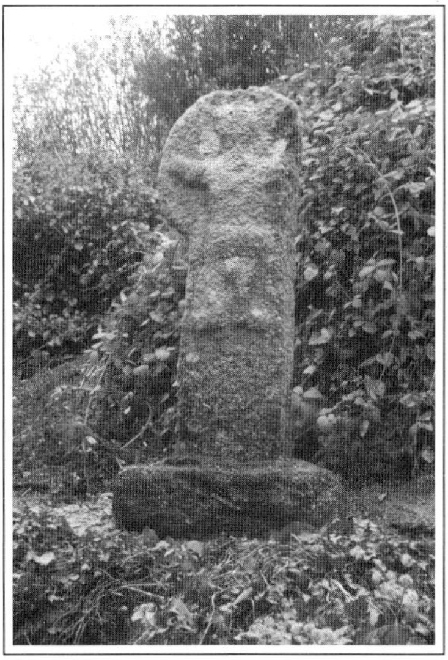

SW 8391 3953 - Situated in the grounds of Trelissick Garden, overlooking the River Fal. Access - On National Trust property: there is no free access, N.T. charges apply.

This granite wheel-headed cross was discovered in a field known as *Park and Grouse,* Cornish for 'Field of the Cross', at Tredrea in the parish of St Erth. The monument was removed to Trelissick by John Davies Gilbert in 1845 and set up in its present site as a landscape feature for his garden. In 1817, Mr Gilbert had also been responsible for removing another cross to a manor house in Eastbourne, Sussex - another property owned by the Gilbert family. The cross at Trelissick has been mutilated, having its head cut down in line with the shaft on one side, which suggests that the old stone may have been used as a gatepost at some time. On the front of the monument is displayed a figure of Christ, portrayed with rather large feet. The reverse face is almost obliterated with only a faint trace remaining of the lower limb of a latin cross running down the shaft. The monument has been erected on a small granite base-stone, on an outcrop of rock sheltered by trees overlooking the river Fal, on the eastern boundary of the estate. In its present position it is dangerous to examine, as there is a sheer drop immediately in front of it. Recently, the National Trust has gained Scheduled Monument Consent to re-position the monument a few feet further back from the cliff edge, so that the cross can be examined in safety. Please see stop press on page 85 for last minute details.

Height 3ft 7 1/2ins (1.105M), width of head 1ft 4 1/2ins (0.42M), width of shaft at neck 11 1/2ins (0.29M), width of shaft at ground 1ft (0.305M), thickness 7 3/4ins to 9 1/2ins (0.195M to 0.24M).

37

Castle Dore Stone, Fowey

INSCRIBED MEMORIAL CROSS

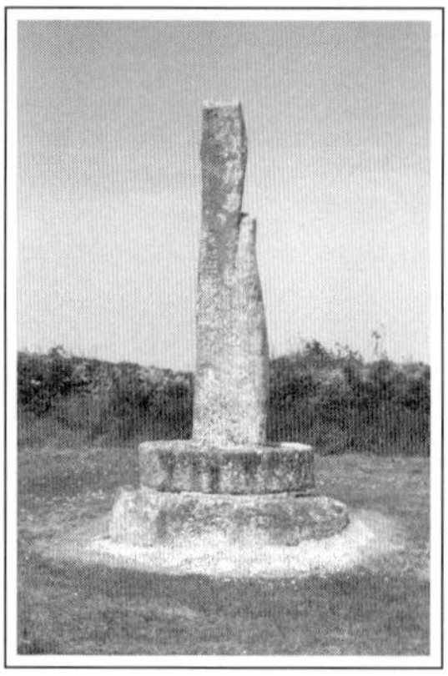

SX 1126 5208 - Situated beside the A3082 road leading to the port of Fowey, 1 mile N.W. of the port. Access - Unlimited.

This large memorial stone was originally situated near the Iron Age hillfort of Castle Dore, and was recorded by Leland in *c*1540, as being a broken cross lying 1 mile south of Castle Dore. Later, the monument appears to have been moved on at least two occasions, and by the 19th century had been set-up outside the northern lodge to Menabilly at Newtown. A plaque commemorating the stone was erected by Fowey Old Cornwall Society in 1961. In 1971, the stone was moved to its present position by Fowey Old Cornwall Society.

On its northern face, the monument displays a Tau Cross, an ancient cross symbol in the shape of the letter 'T'. On the southern face is an inscription in Latin, carved vertically down the shaft. It is extremely worn, but is said to read *DRVSTANVS HIC IACIT CVNOMORI FILIVS*; which translated reads 'Drustanus lies here, son of Cunomorus'. The names Drustanus and Cunomorus have been equated by scholars with the Tristan and King Mark from the famous Arthurian legends. The inscription has been dated to the 6th century. Another unusual feature is that the shaft has a mortice cut into the top of it, similar to the Longcross inscribed stone at St Endellion (North Cornwall no 35). This mortice was intended to receive a cross-head, persumably fixed to the monument at a later date, to transform the inscribed stone into an inscribed cross.

Today, this monument is known under several different names, including the Tristan Stone, Cunomorus Stone or Fowey Longstone.

Height 8ft 9ins (2.67M), width (at top) 1ft 1ins (0.33M), width (at base) 2ft 1ins (0.635M), thickness (at top) 10ins (0.255M), thickness (at base) 1ft 7ins (0.48M).

38

Gerrans Cross, Gerrans

WHEEL-HEADED WAYSIDE CROSS

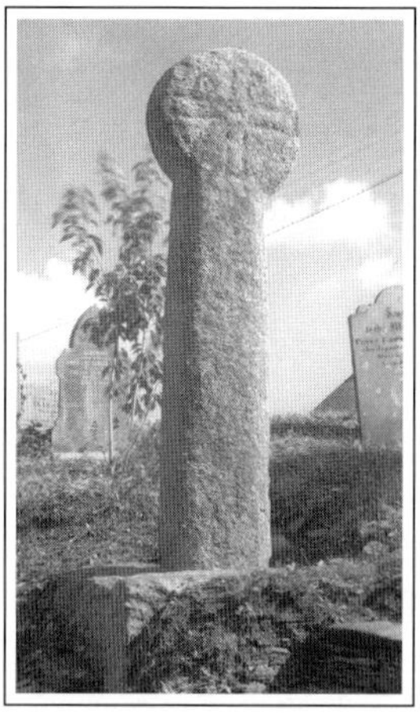

SW 8728 3516 - Situated on the south side of the churchyard, close to the porch. Access - Unlimited.

Prior to 1850, this wheel-headed cross was in use as coping for the churchyard wall, although it does not appear to have suffered as much as the St Teath Cross, (North Cornwall no 95), which was severely mutilated for the same reason. The only adverse effect to the monument appears to be the indistinct crosses, which can only just be discerned on each face. Blight's illustration suggests these were Latin crosses, with the lower limb running down the shaft, although the author could only perceive equal-limbed crosses in very low relief. When the monument was rescued and re-erected, it was set up on a modern base, indicating that the original base-stone had either been lost or more likely, that the cross was removed to the churchyard wall from a nearby church path. The cross is a typical wayside cross rather than a churchyard cross and it is improbable that it originated in the churchyard. This is the only ancient stone cross to be found in the Roseland peninsula, although another cross was recorded in the 1613 parish terrier. Known as Penpirthe Cross, this stood on the boundary between Gerrans and Philleigh parishes.

Height 6ft 8 1/2ins (2.045M), width of shaft at neck 1ft 1 1/2ins (0.34M), width of head 2ft 1ins (0.635M), width of shaft at middle 1ft 2 1/2ins (0.37M), thickness 10ins to 11ins (0.255M to 0.28M).

39

Cross-base inside the church
Kea

CROSS-BASE

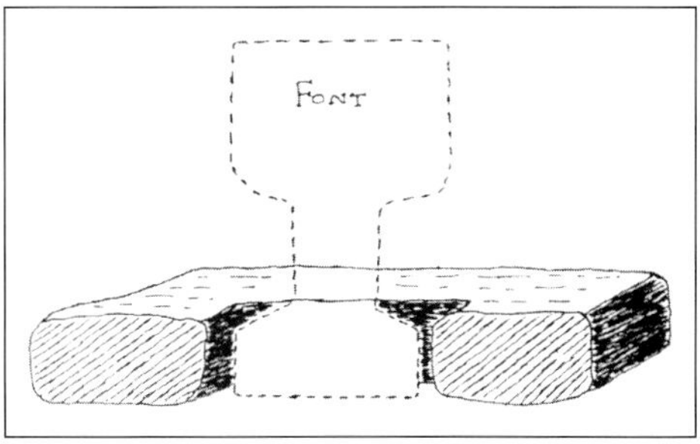

SW 8442 4169 - Inside the Mission Church at Old Kea, which lies 5 miles south of Truro on the west bank of the river Fal. Access - Only when the church is open, normally during daylight hours.

The church at Old Kea, which is situated in the far eastern corner of the parish, was superseded by a modern church near Killiow, in 1802. The old church was demolished soon afterwards, except for the three stage tower. Later in 1863, a small Mission Church was built in the churchyard and the remains of the Kea cross-base placed inside below the font.

The large socketed stone, said to be the base of 'Kea Cross' (see no 40 in this guide), weighed twenty-eight hundredweight when complete, but was later fractured with one half being lost. The granite stone was discovered in a field at Higher Lanner, half a mile west of the churchyard. According to the historian Hals, writing in 1700, a Mr Bawden of Gooderne *c.*1660, found an iron crock full of gold and silver below the monument. The size of the stone and mortice suggests that the monument it supported must have been of massive proportions.

Originally 6ft square (1.83M square), length 6ft (1.83M), width 3ft 3ins (0.99M), thickness 9ins (0.23M), width of mortice 1ft 9ins (0.53M) to fracture.

40

Churchyard cross-shaft
Kea

CHURCHYARD CROSS

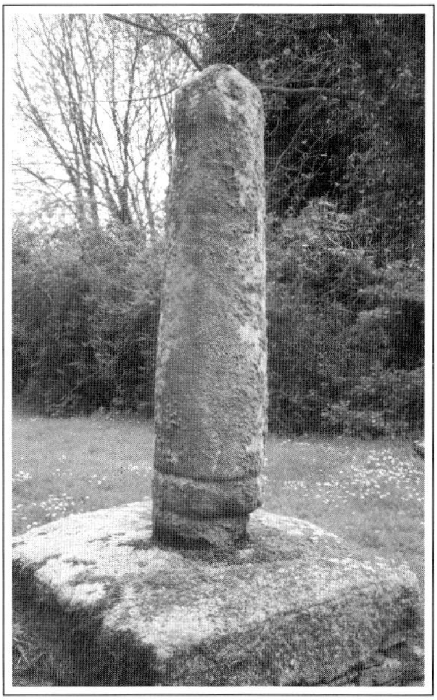

SW 8442 4169 - Situated between the tower of Old Kea church and the small Mission church. Access - Unlimited.

This monument is unusual in being cylindrical in shape, and is set up on an ancient base stone by means of a mortice and tenon joint. The ancient stone was discovered beneath the foundations of the old Poor House, which was demolished when the Mission church was constructed in 1863.

The monument is undecorated except for a raised band running around the shaft a few inches from the base. The only Cornish cross with a similar feature is the Biscovey Stone at St Blazey (see no 10 in this guide), although the latter is more elaborate and inscribed. The cross-head is long lost and all that now remains is a shallow mortice in the top of the shaft to which the head was fixed. Recently, archaeologist Professor Charles Thomas has suggested that this stone could have been a menhir and therefore considerably earlier in date.

Height 5ft 8ins (1.73M), diameter 1ft 2ins (0.355M), base-stone 4ft square (1.22M), base-stone height 11ins (0.28M).

41

Churchyard Cross, Lamorran

GOTHIC LATIN CHURCHYARD CROSS

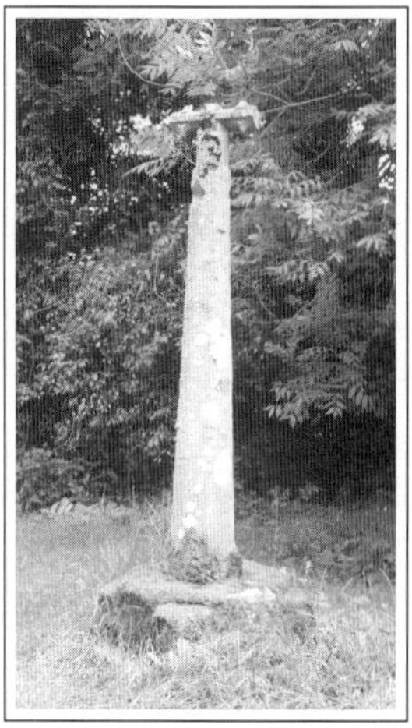

SW 8787 4175 - The monument is situated in Lamorran churchyard, 4 miles south-east of Truro on the eastern side of the River Fal. Access - Unlimited.

This tall, slender cross is cut from a piece of fine-grained Pentewan stone and is supported by a large pedestal of similar material. The monument is a late Gothic style cross with cusps formed between the limbs of the cross-head, and it resembles the Tresallyn cross at St Merryn (North Cornwall no 78). On several occasions during the last century, the head of the monument has been broken off and some historians have recorded the cross complete and others minus its head. The cross-head appears to have been mislaid for a number of years and, according to Henderson, was rediscovered by the Rector under the floor of the church. The cross-head is fixed to the shaft with a small mortice and tenon joint and in 1955 the cross was seen to be missing its upper limb. Later it appears that a modern upper limb was provided but this also has been lost today.

Height 6ft 1ins (1.855M), width of shaft (at neck) 5 3/4ins (0.145M), width of shaft (at base) 10ins (0.255M), base-stone 2ft square (0.61M sq.), height 10ins (0.255M), width of head 1ft 1 3/4ins (0.35M).

42

Churchyard Cross, Lanhydrock

WHEEL-HEADED CHURCHYARD CROSS

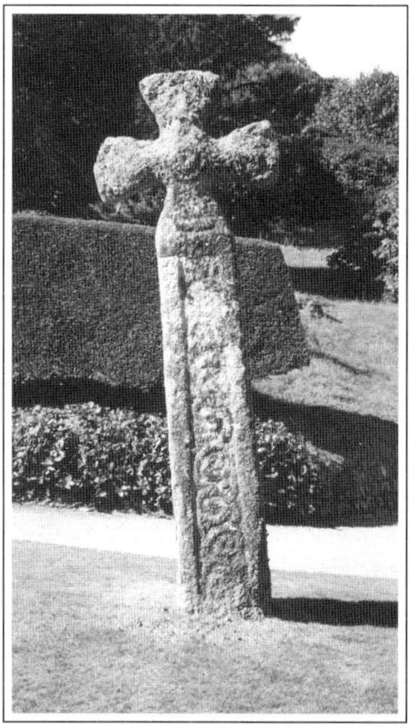

SX 0851 6361 - The cross stands in the parish churchyard at Lanhydrock. Access - Unlimited. There is a public right of way across the National Trust estate, to the Churchyard, from Treffry Gate.

The churchyard at Lanhydrock is within the National Trust estate, with the large mansion situated immediately east of the parish church. The 15th century church is dedicated to St Hydroc and the cross stands on the south-east side of the churchyard, close to the south porch. Originally it was an elaborately decorated wheel-headed four-holed cross but today its head is rather mutilated. Records suggest that the cross lay discarded for many years, and it is thought that during this period the ring which encircled the limbs was broken off and the monument fractured at the neck. There is no documentary evidence as to when, or by whom, the cross was restored, although it was prior to 1850 and was probably commissioned by the Robartes family who formerly owned Lanhydrock House.

The head of the cross is very worn and no decoration can be seen on the limbs. On the front of the head is displayed a central boss, enclosed in a double circular bead and on the reverse face a central boss with a single bead. The shaft, which displays a slight entasis, has four inch wide beads running down the full length of the shaft. On the front of the shaft is figure of eight plaitwork and on the back some fine foliated scrollwork. Traces of decoration can also be seen on the remaining sides, although it is difficult to distinguish due to weathering of the granite.

Height 8ft 1 1/2ins (0.475M), width of head 2ft 7 1/2ins (0.8M), width of shaft (neck) 1ft 1ins (0.33M), width of shaft (near ground) 1ft 6ins (0.46M), thickness of shaft 11ins (0.28M).

43

Treffry Cross, Lanhydrock

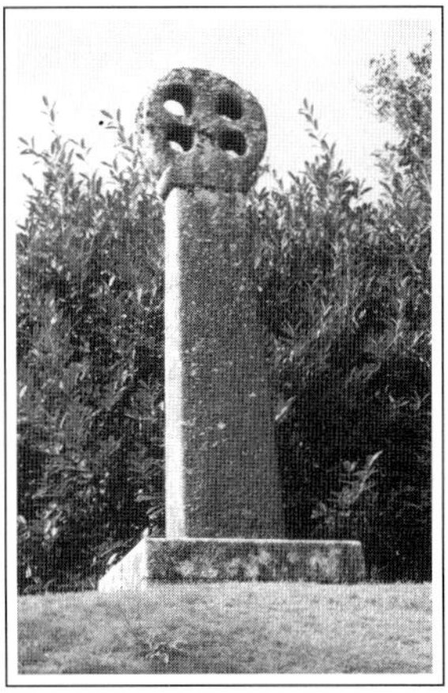

FOUR-HOLED WAYSIDE CROSS

SX 0852 6346 - Situated on a mound at the top of Scotland Hill in the higher gardens in the National Trust's Lanhydrock estate. Access - The cross stands in the National Trust gardens, there is no free access to view the cross. N. T. charges apply.

Visitors to this monument may be surprised to learn that only a small fragment of this large cross is original, that being the upper section of the cross-head. According to Langdon, the fragment was dug out of a hedge at the Treffry crossroads, close to the entrance drive on the western side of the estate, at the instigation of Lord Clifden's brother-in-law, who had shown an interest in the monument. Its location in the hedge had been pointed out to him by the Rev William Iago of Bodmin, in the presence of Langdon and some estate workers, prior to 1896. Langdon later stated that the discovery was rather disappointing, for although only this fragment could be seen in the hedge, it had been hoped that the greater part of the stone was there also, hidden from view. Nevertheless, the fragment was retrieved and later restored on a modern shaft, at Lord Robartes expense, under the direction of Rev Iago. The completed monument was set up in the higher gardens on a mound, and commands extensive views of Lanhydrock estate. No further remains of the monument have ever been discovered to date.

Height of fragment 1ft 8ins (0.51M), width of head 2ft 8ins (0.81M), diameter of holes 7ins (0.18M), Overall height of restored monument, 11ft 7ins (3.53M), thickness 7ins to 9ins (0.18M to 0.23M).

44

Bodwen Cross, Lanhydrock

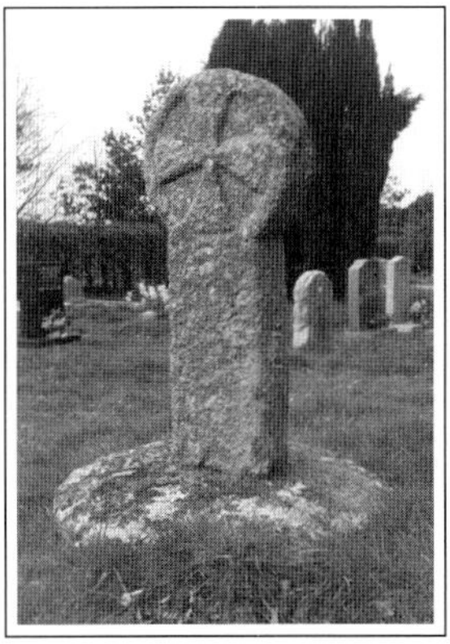

WHEEL-HEADED WAYSIDE CROSS

SX 0862 6417 - In the centre of Lanhydrock cemetery, 1/2 mile due north of Lanhydrock House, and 2 1/2 miles south-east of Bodmin town. Access - Unlimited.

This well-proportioned wayside cross was illustrated by Randolph in 1850, standing in its base-stone near Helman Tor. He also noted that two similar crosses, half buried in soil, could be found at equal distances from it on this ridgeway track. The ancient ridgeway track skirts the slopes of Helman Tor and then runs south-east towards Lanlivery churchtown.

Surprisingly, both Blight and Langdon failed to record this monument; suggesting that the cross was either very well camouflaged or was broken down soon after Hingston's survey. It was in 1937 that the cross was re-discovered by a Mr Pope of Bodwen Farm, built horizontally into a hedge beside the ridgeway track, at approximately SX 0634 6112. The following year, the wayside cross was removed to the new cemetery at Lanhydrock and set up on an old granite millstone at the expense of Lord Robartes. This has been a source of controversy ever since. When its discovery was recorded by Mr. Ashley Rowe in 1937, he stated that it was hoped that the cross would be re-erected as near as possible to where it was found. In 1984, when the Saints' Way footpath from Padstow to Fowey was being set up, Lanlivery parish council made a formal request for the old stone to be returned to Lanlivery and set up on the ridgeway track, which was part of the Saints' Way footpath; unfortunately this request was denied. The monument is cut from a piece of coarse grained moorland granite and displays an equal limbed cross in relief with expanded ends enclosed in a narrow bead. The reverse face is similar.

Height 3ft 9ins (1.14M), width of head 1ft 7 1/2ins (0.495M), width of shaft 1ft (0.305M), thickness of shaft 9ins (0.23M).

45

Trebyan Cross-base, Lanhydrock

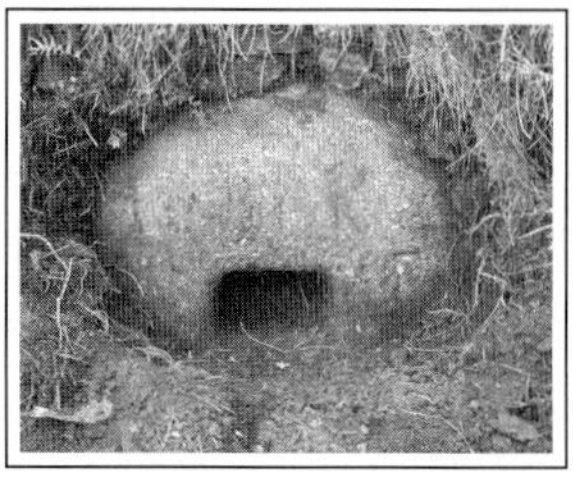

BASE-STONE OF BOUNDARY CROSS

SX 0786 6292 - Built into the foot of a hedge near a junction of a minor road to Fenton Pits and the B3269 Bodmin to Lostwithiel road. Access - Unlimited.

Known as Trebyan cross-base, this coarse-grained granite stone may have once supported the Tredinnick cross, which is no longer extant. The base-stone is 200 metres south of the hamlet of Trebyan and is built into the foot of the hedge on the junction with Tredinnick Lane. The field immediately behind the stone is recorded on the Tithe map of 1840 as Cross Park, suggesting that the stone may be close to its original site. Another reason for suggesting that the stone is near its original position is that the parish boundary between Lanhydrock and Lanlivery runs close to this site and so the cross which the socketed stone supported may have been a boundary cross.

The base-stone is an oval granite stone with a deep mortice cut through it. The most surprising and unusual feature is that it has two inscriptions cut into the granite. Macalister in 1929 translated a small inscription in Latin capitals, carved just above the socket, which read: *MAVISIR* and suggested that if it was ancient, it could date from between the 5th and 6th century. Despite, Macalister's suggestion of an early date for the first inscription, the author considers that the base-stone is more likely to be nearer 12th century than 6th century, as it is of the typical style for a wayside cross. A second inscription, carved RHRK in large letters above the earlier inscription, could represent the initials of a local landowner, the base marking the extent of their lands, these letters are carved above the earlier inscription. On the right hand side of this inscription is carved an Ordnance Survey benchmark.

Width 3ft 7ins (1.09M), mortice 13 1/2ins by 9 1/2ins (0.34M by 0.24M), Height above ground level 2ft 7ins (0.79M).

46

Churchyard Cross (North), Lanivet

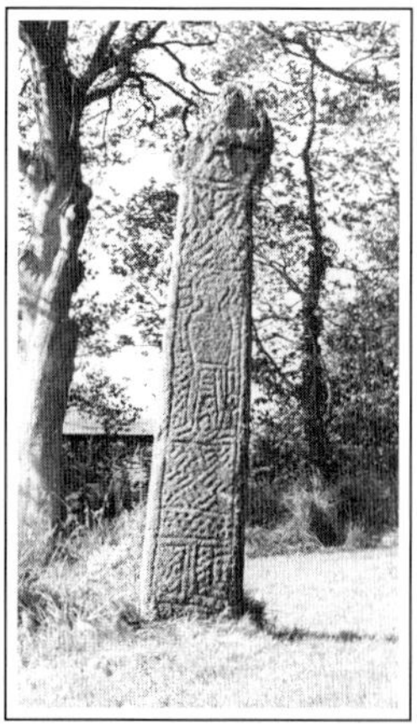

WHEEL-HEADED CHURCHYARD CROSS

SX 0396 6422 - Situated on the north side of the churchyard. Access - Unlimited.

This magnificent monument stands *in situ* and is said to mark the centre of Cornwall, from north to south and east to west. The stone is the most elaborately decorated wheel-cross in the county and, with the exception of two panels of key pattern in relief, consists almost entirely of incised decoration. The cross-head has been badly fractured in the past and today only two thirds of its wheel-head exists. An equal-limbed cross with expanded ends and a central boss is displayed on both faces. The shaft of the cross is well proportioned with a clear entasis on both sides. When examined in 1890, the base-stone was found to be still attached, one foot below the existing ground surface.The decoration on all four sides of the shaft is divided into panels, several of which display rows of putch-dot ornamentation similar to the Connor Downs Cross at Camborne, the Market Cross at Penzance and the Cornish cross now at Eastbourne. The most impressive panel, which is almost three feet high, shows a figure of a man with a tail, the significance of which has never been fully explained, although Dexter suggested it showed pagan influence. Despite the alleged pagan connotations, there are also six panels containing incised crosses; two St Andrew's or diagonal crosses, one equal-limbed cross, two latin crosses and a wheel-headed cross. There are other panels displaying two oval rings crossing each other to form a cross and a panel containing concentric circles.

Height 9ft 7 1/2ins(2.933M), width of head 1ft 10ins (0.56M), width of shaft at the neck 1ft 2ins (0.355M), width of shaft at ground level 1ft 6ins (0.46M).

Churchyard Cross (West) Lanivet

FOUR-HOLED CHURCHYARD CROSS

SX 0392 6421 - Stands on the western side of the parish churchyard. Access - Unlimited.

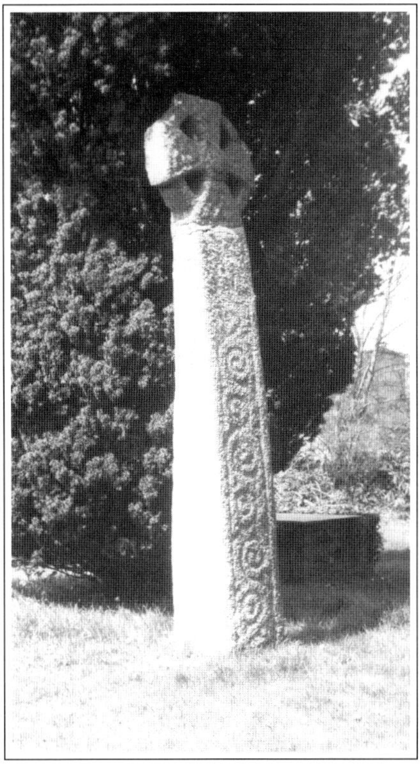

This second elaborate churchyard cross at Lanivet is completely different in style to the cross on the north side of the churchyard (see no 46 in this guide). This tall four-holed cross is *in situ* and is supported by a base-stone now almost hidden from view. It is unusual to find a Cornish churchyard with two ornamented churchyard crosses. The only other churchyard to boast two churchyard crosses is Sancreed in West Penwith (see West Penwith nos 81 and 82). At Sancreed, one can clearly see that one churchyard cross is later and partly modelled on the earlier one. At Lanivet, there is no similarity in artistic design or sculpture between the two crosses. The only fact that connects them is that they are both in the same churchyard, and there is no evidence to suggest that they did not both originate there.

The cross-head, which at some time was fractured from its shaft, displays triquetra knots on all four limbs enclosed in a narrow bead with a central boss. The reverse face of the head is similar, and also displays triquetra knots on its limbs. The limbs of the head are not symmetrical and are square at the ends, rather than rounded in line with the outer ring. The front (east) face of the shaft displays some good foliated scrollwork, while on the western face there is double-beaded interlace, consisting of figure of eight knots. On the southern side of the shaft is more foliated scrollwork, and on the northern side some poorly executed plaitwork. The decoration on the upper part of the cross-shaft, is very worn on both faces, suggesting that at some stage in the monument's history, it has been misused, perhaps at the time when the cross was fractured at the neck? Today, the monument is threatened more by the Yew tree directly behind it, than any other risk. The tree is continously rubbing against the monument, and in time will damage the decoration. Photographs in the author's posession show that the tree was planted after 1938, at which time the cross stood clearly visible from all sides. The author hopes that in the future the Yew tree can be trimmed, or removed and replaced with a smaller one.

Height 10ft 6ins (3M), width of shaft at the neck 1ft 4 1/2ins (0.42M), width of shaft at ground level 1ft 6ins (0.47M).

48

Bodwannick Cross, Lanivet

WHEEL-HEADED WAYSIDE CROSS

SX 0371 6561 - Situated in the garden of Bodwannick Manor, which is 1 mile due north of Lanivet churchtown. Access - The cross is on private grounds; there is no public access.

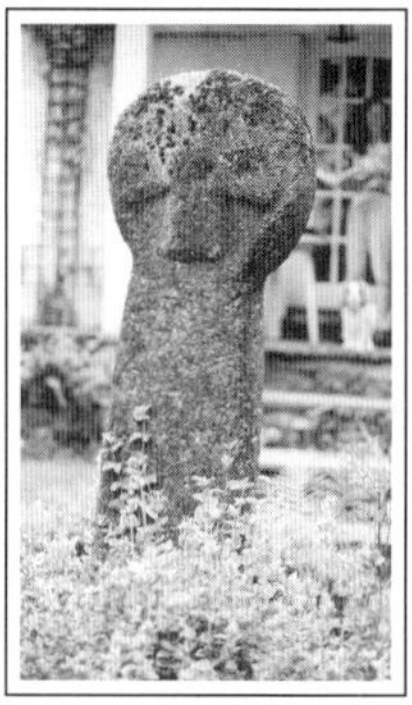

According to Langdon, this cross was discovered by Mr Richard Knight, who farmed Bodwannick in the 1890s. At this time the monument was in use as a gatepost and buried head-down in the ground. At Langdon's request, Mr Knight had the cross unearthed for examination, and the illustration in *Old Cornish Crosses* shows the gate hangings still attached. What is surprising is that Mr Knight re-buried the cross on Langdon's departure and continued using it as a gatepost for another thirty years. When first seen by Henderson it was still in this absurd position. He later recorded that it had been restored by Mr Lyne, a new owner of Bodwannick, on a modern concrete base-stone in the front garden close to the manor house. In the late 1970s the stone was again shifted within the garden when the owner built a verandah on the front of the house. At this time the concrete base-stone was removed and the cross set directly into the ground with granite stones placed around it to form a base.

The monument displays an equal-limbed cross with expanded ends in relief and a small hole in the centre on both faces. A bead surrounds the head linking the ends of the limbs. On the front of the shaft, just below the lower limb, is an incised line which runs horizontally across the shaft and down each side, forming a bead. On the reverse the shaft is plain. The iron gate hangings have been removed and the holes cemented over.

Height 5ft 7ins (1.7M), width of head 1ft 10ins (0.56M), width of shaft at the neck 1ft (0.305M), width of shaft at ground level 1ft 4ins (0.41M).

49

Reperry Cross, Lanivet

WHEEL-HEADED WAYSIDE CROSS

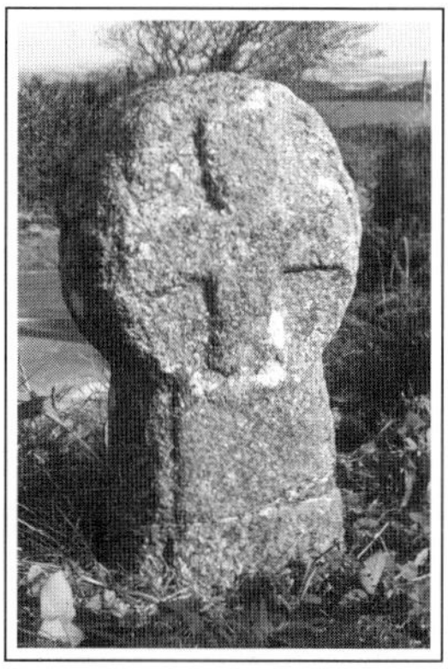

SX 0464 6331 - Situated in a hedge at the intersection of six ancient tracks, 1 mile south-east of Lanivet churchtown. Access - Unlimited.

The first reference to Reperry Cross is an engraving in the Gentleman's Magazine of 1805, but after this the monument appears to have disappeared. Blight recorded it as missing, with only the base-stone remaining. Blight did however note that another cross existed at St Ingunger, built into the garden wall. This later prompted Henderson to search for the stone, which on discovery, he compared with the engraving of 1805 and concluded that it was the lost Reperry Cross. Meanwhile, during this interim period, the landowner, Sir Robert Edgcumbe, had commissioned a replica cross which was placed in the ancient base-stone. A plaque set in the hedge to this day reads *Reperry Cross, Restored by Sir Robert Edgcumbe*, although this actually refers to the replica. In 1926, the original cross was returned to its former site and the replica removed to private ground near Reperry Manor, at the expense of Lord Clifden of Lanhydrock. On April 30th 1993, an attempt was made to steal the cross. It was dragged off the hedge and abandoned in the road, but later re-erected on October 5th 1993. In January 1997, the hedge below the monument was severely damaged by a vehicle, threatening the stability of the cross, but it was later re-built during April 1997 by the County Council under the supervision of Mr David Stark.

Height 4ft (1.22M), width of head 1ft 7ins (0.48M), width of shaft at the neck 1ft 1in (0.33M).

50

St Ingunger Cross, Lanivet

WHEEL-HEADED WAYSIDE CROSS

SX 0597 6334 - Situated south of the A30 Bodmin bypass on an ancient road linking Lanivet churchtown and Lanhydrock, at a junction with a road to Fentonpits. Access - Unlimited.

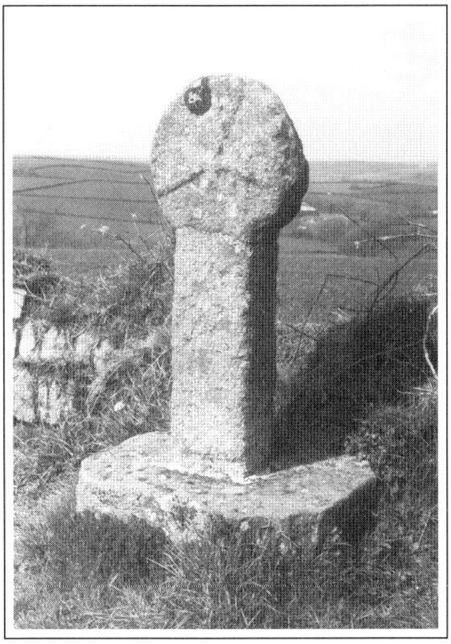

This granite wayside cross appears to be one of a series which marked ancient routes from Lanivet to Lanlivery and Lanivet to Lanhydrock. There is no other parish in mid Cornwall where there are four almost complete wayside crosses within the distance of one and a half miles. The St Ingunger cross has been moved on at least two occasions, from one side of the road junction to the other. In 1926, the monument was set back from the road in a recess in the hedge by Lanhydrock estate workers. Because its base-stone was missing, a substantial new granite slab was utilised to support the cross.
The cross-head displays a widely expanded equal-limbed cross on the front, its lower limb expanded to the width of the shaft. No bead is visible and the limbs, cut in relief, stretch to the edge of the head. The reverse face also displays an equal-limbed cross, but with much narrower limbs. The monument was fractured at the neck at the end of the 19th century.
This cross may have been set up for a dual function, to mark the ancient route to Lanlivery (now part of the Saints' Way footpath), and also to indicate a path to the nearby site of St Ingunger's ancient chapel and holywell. Today, no visible evidence remains of either site. The field immediately behind the cross (north) is recorded as 'Cross Park' in the Tithe Apportionment map of 1839.

Height 4ft 4 1/2ins (1.33M), width of head 1ft 10ins (0.56M), width of shaft 1ft (0.305M), thickness 8ins (0.2M).

51

Fenton Pits Cross, Lanivet

WHEEL-HEADED WAYSIDE CROSS

SX 0610 6297 - Situated in the small scattered hamlet of Fenton Pits a 1/2 mile south of St Ingunger Cross. Access - Unlimited.

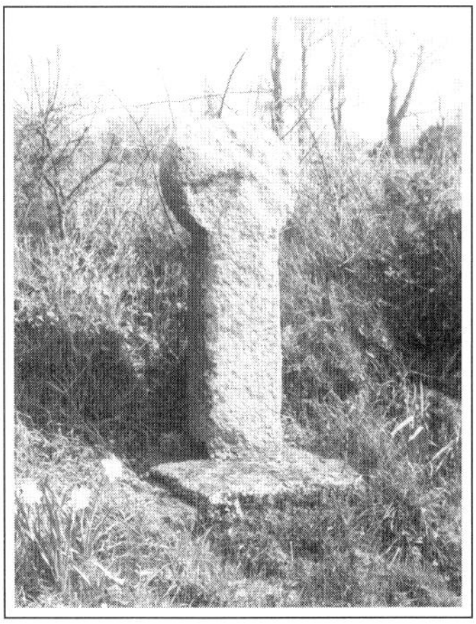

When seen at the end of the 19th century, this cross had been extensively damaged. The shaft had been fractured and the cross, with a short piece of shaft, had been set in the ground, with the remaining portion of the monument still firmly set in its base-stone nearby. The cross-head has also received a great deal of damage over the centuries, with the upper limb and one of the horizontal limbs almost lost due to years of neglect.
Records suggest that this cross, along with other neighbouring crosses on this ancient route to Lanlivery, were all restored during the 1920s by workmen from the Lanhydrock estate. This was largely thanks to Henderson's survey of the Lanivet crosses and his encouragement of a restoration programme. The cross is similar in style to the St Ingunger Cross except for the addition of a narrow bead joining the extremities of the cross limbs. The restoration of the monument is excellent and it takes a keen eye to identify where the cross-shaft was originally fractured.

Height 4ft 3 1/2ins (1.31M), width of head 1ft 11 1/2ins (0.6M), width of shaft 1ft 1 1/2ins (0.34M), thickness 9 1/2ins (0.24M).

52

Lesquite Cross, Lanivet

WHEEL-HEADED WAYSIDE CROSS

SX 0665 6268 - Situated 1/2 mile south-east of Fenton Pits cross at the entrance drive to Lesquite Farm. Access - Unlimited.

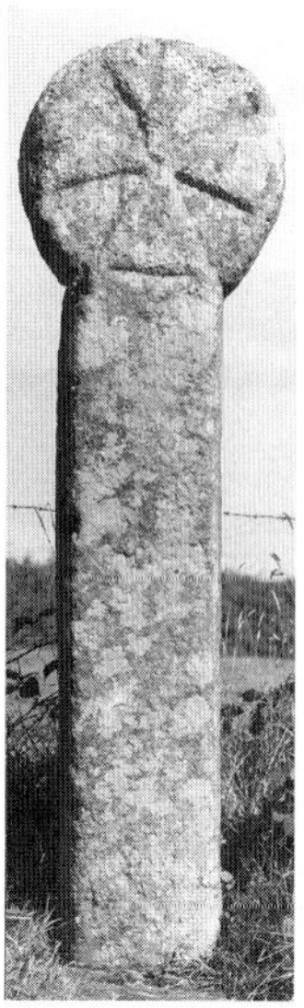

This fine wheel-headed cross has been recorded under several different names. When illustrated by Blight in 1858 he called it Fenton Pits Cross and only mentioned the existence of a second cross, which today is known as the Fenton Pits Cross (see no 51 in this guide). In 1885, the cross was removed to St Breward parish by a Mr Collins and set up in his private garden at Lanke, together with two additional crosses which still remain there, (see North Cornwall no's 15 and 16). Here the cross was recorded by Langdon and named Lanke no 1. It had been placed directly in the ground owing to the fact that the base-stone was left at Lesquite.

It was not until 1926 that the monument was brought back to Lanivet parish and returned to its original base-stone. This was no doubt due to the influence of Lord Clifden and the Lanhydrock estate. The cross is again similar to the Fenton Pits Cross, having a bead joining the extremities of the limbs, made by cutting four triangular segments out of the cross-head. Although the front face of the monument is well executed, the reverse is far cruder, as if the stonemason had rushed the work. This is the tallest wayside cross in Lanivet parish and the most well preserved, complete with its base-stone.

Height 7ft 4ins (2.235M), width of head 2ft (0.61M), width of shaft 1ft 3ins (0.38M), thickness 11ins (0.28M).

53

Treliggan Cross, Lanivet

WHEEL-HEADED WAYSIDE CROSS

SX 0557 6411 - Situated 1 mile due east of Lanivet churchtown and 3/4 mile north-west of Reperry Cross. Access - The cross is on private ground; there is no public access.

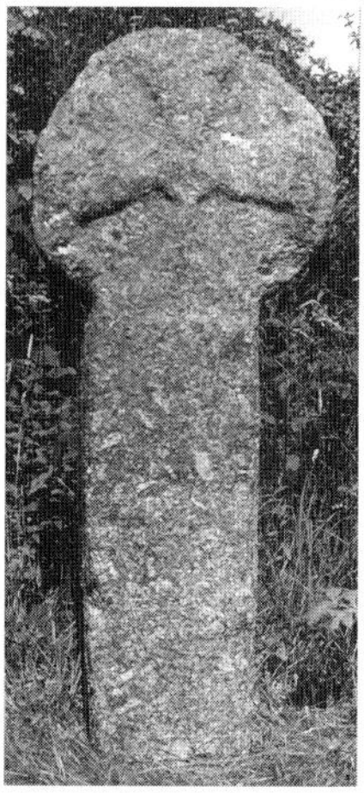

This fine wayside cross was discovered in May 1956 by Mr T. Williams, a former owner of Treliggan Farm, in use as a gatepost. It was later removed to the garden of the farmhouse at Treliggan and re-erected there for preservation, still complete with iron gate hinges. When discovered, the stone measured 7 feet 2 inches in height but, due to being set up directly in the ground without a base-stone, the overall height is now considerably less.

The cross differs slightly in style from its neighbouring Lanivet crosses. This example displays an equal-limbed cross with expanded ends which terminate in a central lozenge shaped disc, rather than a central boss; the extremities of the cross-limbs are joined together with a narrow limb. The reverse face is similar. The shaft has a noticeable entasis and a bead running down each side. Another unusual feature is a faint incised square panel containing an incised St Andrew's Cross, now barely discernible on the front of the shaft.

As the monument had been in use as a gatepost for many years, it is not possible to pin-point its original site, although the consensus of opinion between local historians is that it probably marked the junction between the track from Reperry Cross and the road west to the churchtown. Here, where the two roads meet, is a field known as Cross Park in the Tithe Apportionment map of 1839.

Height (to ground level) 4ft 8ins (1.42M), width of head 1ft 10ins (0.56M), width of shaft (at neck) 1ft (0.305M), width of shaft (at ground level) 1ft 1ins (0.33M), thickness 10ins to 11 1/2ins (0.255M to 0.29M).

54

Laninval Cross, Lanivet

WHEEL-HEADED WAYSIDE CROSS

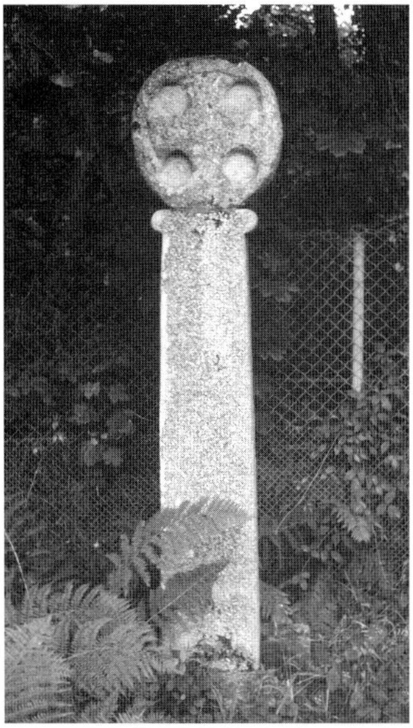

SX 0495 6566 - Stands in the grounds of Laninval House on the eastern side of the house. Laninval is on the A389 Lanivet to Bodmin road. Access - The cross is on private grounds; there is no public access.

This unusual cross-head was discovered built into a shed at the rear of premises in Higher Bore Street, Bodmin, by a former owner, Mr H. Dennis. He had the stone removed to Laninval House, a family home, and erected on a modern shaft and base-stone at the rear of the property. In 1956, Ellis recorded that according to the then owner of the Bodmin property the cross-shaft still existed but had been built into a wall and plastered over and was no longer visible.

The cross-head is unique among Cornish crosses. It is roughly circular and consists of four round depressions enclosed in a bead, which so positioned form an equal-limbed cross. The reverse face is similar but the bead is omitted. Ellis suggested that the cross-head may have been a cresset stone, although Mary Henderson noted that the cup marks or depressions would not then have been required on both sides. If the stone was a cresset stone there would have been no reason for a bead either. Cresset stones seen by the author appear to have much deeper holes than on this monument.

Width of head 1ft 7 ins (0.48M), thickness 10ins (0.255M), diameter of depressions 5 1/2ins (0.14M).

55

Tremore Cross, Lanivet

WHEEL-HEADED WAYSIDE CROSS

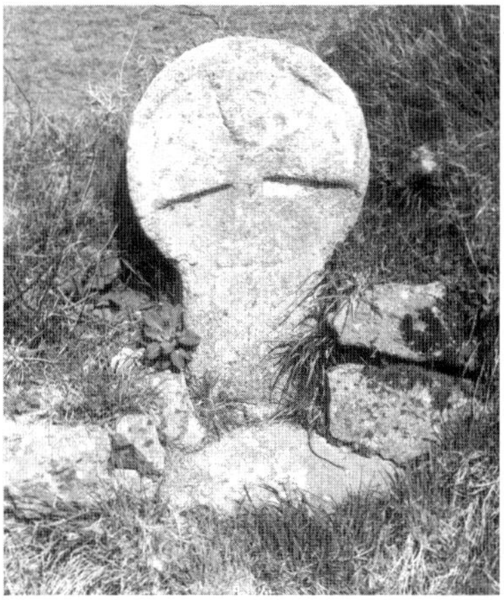

SX 0208 6506 - Situated on the northern side of a staggered crossroad; 1 1/2 miles north-west of Lanivet churchtown. Access - Unlimited.

This cross takes its name from the hamlet of Tremore (Tremoor) which is situated half a mile west of the crossroads. Throughout most of the 19th century the cross, with its base-stone, straddled a gap in the hedge, which acted as a culvert for water draining from the field behind. Since this period, the road level has been raised considerably, so that on approaching the crossroads today, the cross is not immediately visible.

Originally the cross would have been a great deal taller, but a portion of its shaft has been lost. The monument's former position would have probably been in the centre of the crossroads. Owing to the lack of a tenon on the bottom of the shaft, the mortice in the base-stone must have been enlarged to receive the complete width of the cross-shaft, which runs completely through the base-stone.

The cross is a well proportioned example, displaying an equal-limbed cross with expanded ends, enclosed in a narrow bead, the ends of which extend down the edge of the shaft on both sides. The reverse face is similar. There are two crosses in the neighbourhood which closely resemble this monument: the Rectory Cross at Withiel and the newly discovered Lamorrick Cross (see nos 100 and 58 in this guide).

Height 3ft 4ins (1.105M), width of shaft 1ft 3ins (0.38M), width of head 2ft 2ins (0.66M), thickness 9ins (0.23M), base-stone width 3ft 6ins (1.605M), thickness 1ft (0.305M).

56

Woodley Cross, Lanivet

WHEEL-HEADED WAYSIDE CROSS

SX 0270 6395 - Stands beside the Old Coach Road, which runs south-west from the hamlet of Lamorrick to the A30 trunk road. Access - Unlimited.

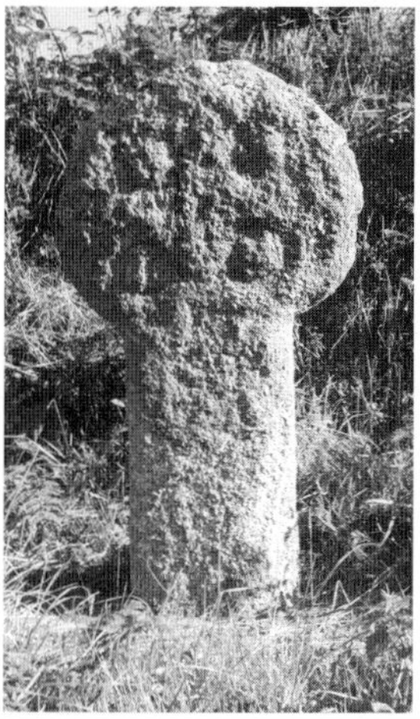

Woodley cross was first recorded by Langdon in 1896, lying by the side of a rough track, with a portion of its base-stone nearby. By the 1920s, Charles Henderson recorded that the cross had been adopted as a gatepost and all knowledge of its whereabouts was later lost. In 1972, with the help of Mr Sandercock of Higher Cadwin Farm, Mary Henderson re-discovered the cross, lying in the corner of a field. Unfortunately the cross was not rescued at this time and became covered again in undergrowth. Later, through the efforts of Liz Briggs and Bodmin Old Cornwall Society, the monument was retrieved and re-erected on the Old Coach Road on the 10th September 1983.

In May 1986, the cross was shifted, along the Old Coach Road to the junction with Clann Lane (NGR SX 0321 6432), thus bringing it in line with the newly publicised Saints' Way footpath from Padstow to Fowey. When villagers and members of the Old Cornwall Society realised that the cross had been moved without any consultation, they complained bitterly to Cornwall County Highways who had the stone reinstated on its former site six weeks later.

On each side of the head are four triangular depressions, which so positioned, form the outline of a cross.

Height 3ft 6ins (1.065M), width of head 1ft11 1/2ins (0.595M), width of shaft 12 1/2ins (0.32M), thickness (at neck) 8 1/2ins (0.215M), thickness (at base) 9 1/2ins (0.24M).

57

St Benet's Cross, Lanivet

WHEEL-HEADED CROSS possibly a GABLE CROSS

SX 0384 6366 - In the front garden of St Benet's Abbey Hotel and Restaurant. The property stands beside the A389 road, 1/2 mile due south of Lanivet churchtown. Access - The monument is situated on private ground but can be easily viewed from beside the public highway.

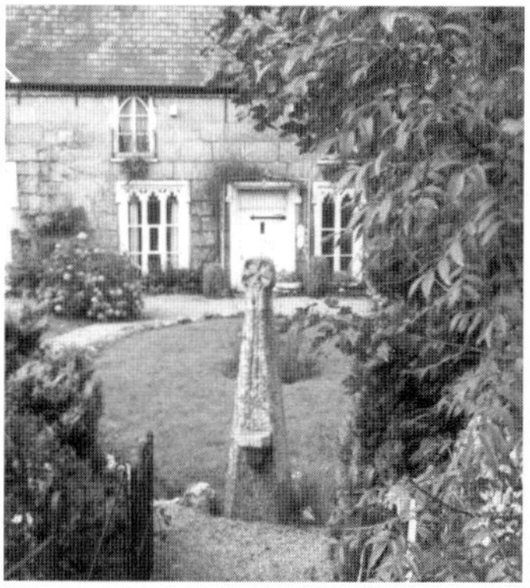

The site of St Benet's Hotel dates from the early 15th century and is believed to have been a Lazar house, or hospital, rather than an Abbey or Priory. The monument in question stands in front of the house, close to the roadside, and is mounted on a modern shaft of most inappropriate proportions.

The origin of this small round-headed granite cross is unknown. The cross on each side of the head is formed by four triangular depressions cut to display the symbol in relief. Below it at the neck can be seen a small incised Latin cross enclosed in a bead, which runs down to join the modern tapered shaft. The tapered shaft is also cut from granite and has chamfered angles and a drinking bowl or bird bath near its base. An iron bracket runs down the back of the monument, clamping the original cross head to its modern shaft.

In the author's opinion the size of the cross-head eliminates it from being a free-standing cross and he considers it more likely to have been a gable cross from the ancient chapel of St Benet's, of which the tower part survives today.

Height 1ft 5 3/4ins (0.45M), width of head 11ins (0.28M), thickness 8 1/2ins (0.215M), total height 7ft 5 3/4ins (2.28M).

58

Lamorrick Cross
Lanivet

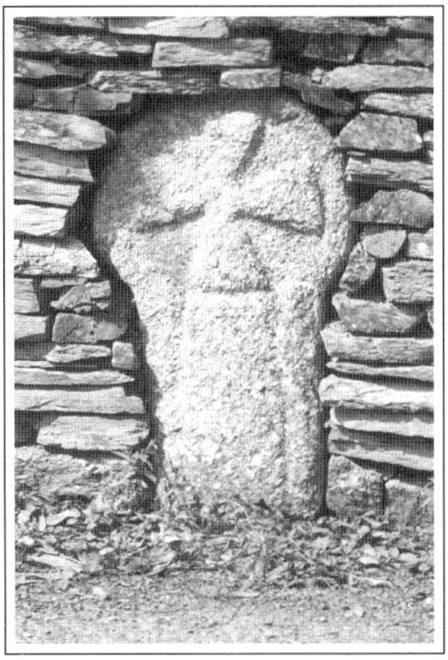

WHEEL-HEADED WAYSIDE CROSS

SX 0357 6460 - In a garden wall at the hamlet of Lamorrick, 1/4 mile north-west of Lanivet churchtown. Access - Unlimited, can be viewed from the public road.

This well preserved cross minus a portion of its shaft, was discovered on July 30th 1991 built horizontally into the foundation of a cottage garden hedge at Lamorrick, by the owner Mr Burden and his son. A search for the remaining piece of shaft and its base-stone amongst the stone rubble from the hedge, proved unsuccessful. The cross must have lain at the bottom of the hedge for a considerable time. Mr Burden's family had owned the property since 1935 and this was the first time the hedge had been rebuilt in that time. The wayside cross is very similar in design to the Tremore Cross (see no 55 in this guide), and displays an equal-limbed cross with expanded ends on each face. A narrow bead runs around the head on both sides, the ends of which continue down the length of the shaft.

The site of the discovery is beside an old track which runs north to Bodwannick Manor. This track, which eventually narrows to a footpath near Bodwannick, was the original church path from the village of Nanstallon, via Lamorrick to the churchtown, and originally the cross must have marked this route. In 1929, another cross was discovered at Hooper's Bridge near the northern end of this path and is preserved in the gardens of Bodwannick Manor (see no 48 in this guide). On Sunday 13th October 1991, the Bodmin Old Cornwall Society organised a re-dedication ceremony for the Lamorrick Cross.

Height 3ft 1ins (0.94M), width of head 1ft 10ins (0.56M), width of shaft 1ft 2ins to 1ft 3 1/2ins (0.355M to 0.395M), thickness 7 1/2ins (0.19M.

59

Trethew Cross
Lanlivery

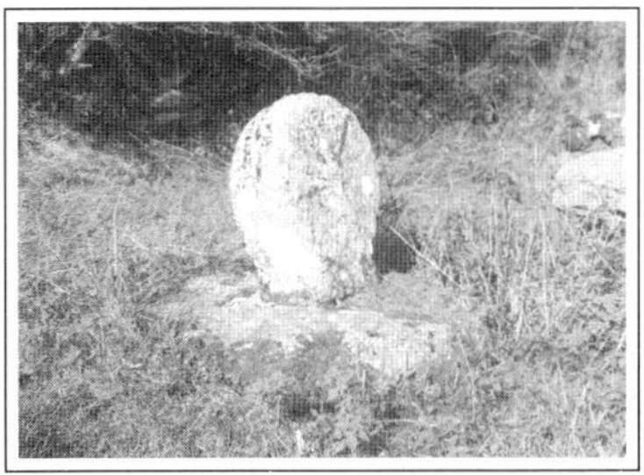

WHEEL-HEADED WAYSIDE CROSS

SX 0735 5881 Situated on a church path leading S.W. from Lanlivery churchtown, 1/2 mile SW of Roselath Farm. Access - Unlimited, the church path is a public footpath.

This old granite cross-head was discovered by the Rev W. E. Wynne, vicar of Lanlivery in 1900, and was illustrated by Langdon in 1906. The base-stone is *in situ*, marking the church path from the parish of Luxulyan, east via the farms of Gready and Roselath to Lanlivery. The cross-head is a large solid-looking stone of considerable weight, with a short portion of shaft fixed to its base-stone with a cement joint. Twenty years ago, this cross lay loose on the ground, near the base, but was later re-fixed to its base.

The cross-head displays an equal-limbed cross with expanded ends to its limbs and is cut in relief; there is a small raised circle instead of a boss in the centre of the cross-limbs. The reverse face is similar. The field in which the monument is situated is recorded on the Tithe map of 1841 as 'Cross Mould'.

Height 2ft 5ins (0.735M), width of head 1ft 11ins (0.585M), width of shaft 1ft 2 1/2ins (0.37M), Thickness 8 1/2ins (0.215M).

60

Trevorry or Sandyway Cross, Lanlivery

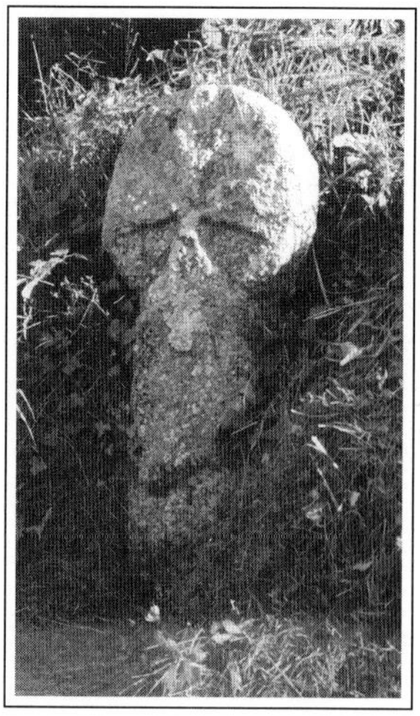

WHEEL-HEADED WAYSIDE CROSS

SX 0791 5796 - Situated 1 mile south of Lanlivery churchtown at a narrow road junction. Access - Unlimited.

This cross was discovered in 1936 during road alterations at the junction of two country lanes. A large granite boulder with a round hole in it, was found at the same time and utilized as the base-stone when re-erected by the Council Council. In 1940, the monument was hit by an army lorry and was re-erected again in September 1941, under the supervision of Rev Wynne, vicar of Lanlivery.

On the night of the 21st January 1990, the cross was stolen, leaving its base-stone empty. Villagers, led by local historian Eric Higgs and councillor Howard Roberts, started an immediate search of the parish. The police were informed and the author provided photographs and a detailed description of the cross. Appeals were broadcast by local radio and television in the hope that the monument would be returned. Later in March 1990, the cross was retrieved by the police from a private garden in an adjoining parish. On June 4th 1990, the cross was re-erected at its former site, and was re-dedicated by the Bishop of Truro, the Rt Rev Michael Ball, assisted by the Rev David Keighley, vicar of Lanlivery.

Height 3ft 5ins (1.04M), width of head 1ft 5ins (0.43M), width of shaft (at neck) 10ins (0.255M), width of shaft (at base) 11 1/2ins (0.29M), thickness 7ins (0.18M).

61

Menawink Cross, Lanlivery

WHEEL-HEADED WAYSIDE CROSS

SX 0711 5959 - Situated on the southern side of Helman Tor, where the old ridgeway track joins the road from Crift to Lanlivery churchtown. Access - Unlimited.

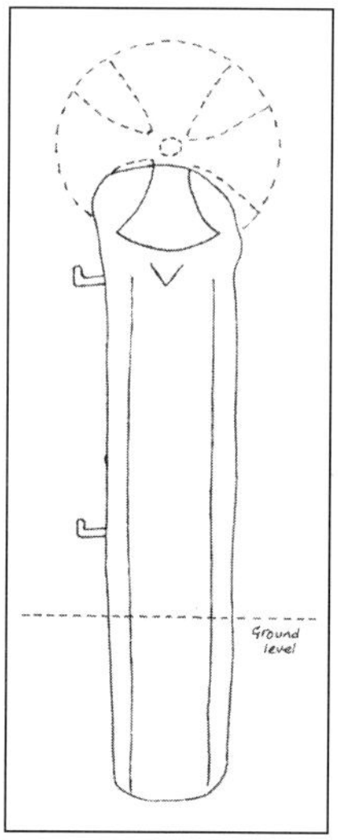

In October 1990, the author was shown this mutilated cross by Eric Higgs of Lanlivery, in use as a gatepost at the entrance of a field known as 'Cross Park'. In 1850, historian Randolph illustrated Bodwen Cross (see no 44 in this guide) on the old ridgeway track and in a footnote stated '*at almost equal distances from it on the same road are two similar crosses, buried halfway up in the soil'*. In the author's opinion this is one of those missing crosses. To facilitate its use as a gatepost, part of the head had been hacked off, so that all that now exists of the cross-head is an incised outline of the lower limb of a Maltese style cross. The shaft displays a narrow bead running down its full length on both sides, with, unusually, an incised 'V' cut just below the neck. Mr King, the landowner, stated that the gatepost (cross) was shifted in approximately 1980 from the opposite side of the parish road to its site of discovery, five metres to the north.

On Saturday 3rd November 1990, the Menawink Cross was re-erected by local farmer Mr David Chapman, with his sons and workmen, in the presence of the author, Mr Higgs, the Rev Keighley and local parishioners. On Good Friday 1991, it was re-dedicated by the Rev David Keighley, vicar of Lanlivery, in a ceremony witnessed by over sixty local people.

Height 7ft 1ins (2.16M), width of head (existing) 1ft 7ins (0.48M), width of shaft 1ft 6ins (0.46M), thickness of shaft 9ins (0.23M).

62

Churchyard Cross, Lostwithiel

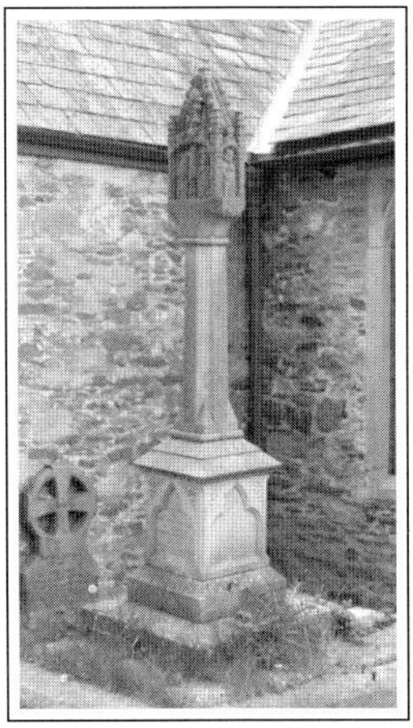

GOTHIC LANTERN CROSS

SX 1043 5979 - On the south side of St Bartholomews church at Lostwithiel. Access - Unlimited.

The original site of this fine lantern cross-head of Pentewan stone, discovered in the 19th century, is not known.
In 1882, the cross-head was erected on a modern octagonal shaft and stepped base-stone, also cut from Pentewan stone, and set up in the churchyard. The restoration of the monument was commissioned by Francis Margery Hext of Trenarren, to a design drawn-up by the Rev William Iago of Bodmin. The cross now marks a private tomb to a member of the Hext family.
The south face of the cross depicts a scene of the Crucifixion, while the north face shows the Virgin Mary and Child; on the eastern face is carved a figure of a Crowned King holding a sceptre in one hand and an Orb in the other. The remaining western face depicts St Bartholomew holding a flaying knife in his right hand. The flaying knife is the recognised symbol of St Bartholomew, who was martyred by being skinned alive.

Height of cross head 2ft 7ins (0.79M), width 1ft 1 3/4ins (0.35M), thickness 7 1/2ins (0.19M), total height of restored monument 5ft 8ins (1.73M).

63

Crewel Cross, Lanlivery

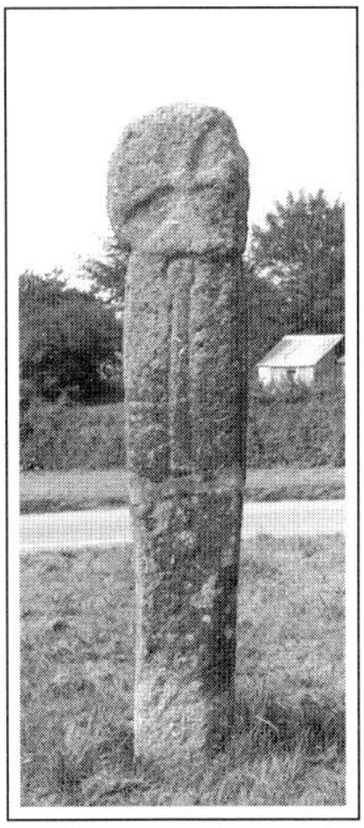

WHEEL-HEADED WAYSIDE CROSS

SX 0893 5909 - Situated on a grass island at the junction of the B2269 Bodmin to Fowey road, with the A390 St Austell to Liskeard road. Access - Unlimited.

In 1870, this mutilated cross was first reported, built into a stile in two sections,on the nearby church path from Lanlivery to Lostwithiel. The upper portion of shaft and cross-head was used as the stride bar of the stile, with the remaining piece of shaft being used as a step.
Through the enthusiasm of Mr Richard Foster of Lawithan, these two stones were removed from the stile in September 1900 and reunited with the aid of metal pins. The base-stone could not be found so another block of weathered granite was utilized for this purpose and the restored cross set up on the green outside a row of cottages known as 'No Mans Land'.
The cross-head displays a widely expanded equal-limbed cross in relief on both faces. A small segment of the head had been hacked off while the stone was in use as part of the stile. The shaft displays a double incised line extending from the lower limb of the cross, down the centre of the shaft to terminate in a circle midway. A similar design can be seen on the crosses at Tregaminion, Tywardreath (see no 90 in this guide), and also on the Tregullow Cross, now at Heanton Punchardon churchyard in North Devon (see page 14 in this guide).
The reverse face of the shaft is unworked, and badly damaged, with one edge being chamfered off while in use as a step for the stile. Although the original height of the wayside cross may have been up to 11feet, today the monument measures 9 feet 2 inches after restoration, 15inches being used to form a new tenon for the base-stone. The remainder was lost when the two portions of shaft were squared off, prior to fixing.

Height 9ft 2ins (2.79M), width of head 1ft 11ins (0.585M), width of shaft(at middle) 1ft 8ins (0.51M), (at ground level) 1ft 4ins (0.405M), thickness 9ins to 10 1/2ins (0.23M to 0.265M).

64

Three Stiles Cross
Luxulyan

WHEEL-HEADED WAYSIDE CROSS

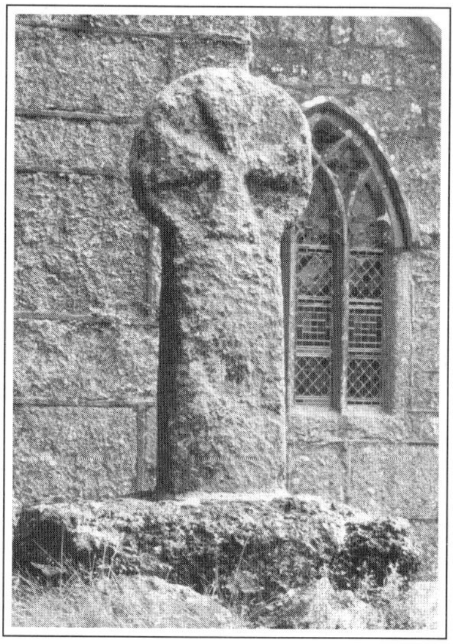

SX 0521 5807 - Situated at the lychgate on the south-west side of Luxulyan churchyard. Luxulyan churchtown is 5 miles north-east of St Austell. Access - Unlimited.

This cross was rescued from a place known as Three Stiles on the old road from Bodmin near Consence by the Rev R. G. Grylls, vicar of Luxulyan from 1813 to 1853. The cross was moved to the vicarage and set up on a rockery in the garden, and remained here until about 1890, when it was removed to its present site by the church gate. On the shaft, there are holes suggesting it was once used as a gatepost; this may have been the excuse for 'rescuing it'. The monument displays an equal-limbed cross in relief with expanded ends enclosed in a narrow bead. The reverse face is similar and the shaft is plain. It is supported by a base-stone of the striking local pink and black granite known as Luxulyanite, while its original socket is said to be still built into a hedge at its former site. Langdon's illustration of 1896 shows a tenon on the end of the shaft, indicating that its height was never any more than five feet.

Height 4ft 4 1/2ins (1.335M), width of head 1ft 11 1/2ins (0.595M), width of shaft 1ft 3ins (0.38M), thickness 8 1/2ins (0.215M).

65

Trevellan Cross
Luxulyan

WHEEL-HEADED WAYSIDE CROSS

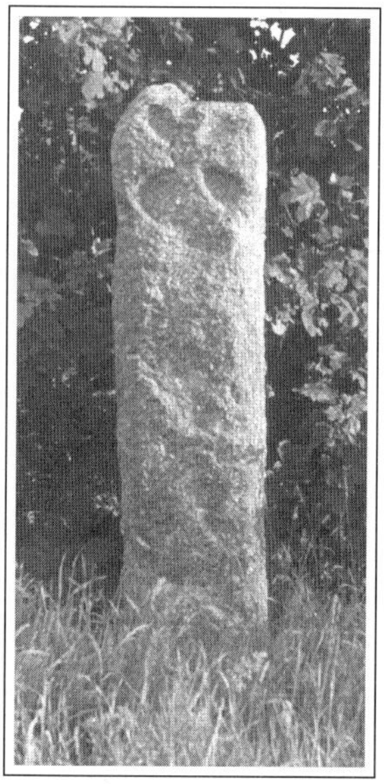

SX 0319 6131 - Situated at Lockengate on the A391 road from Innis Downs to St Austell. Access - Unlimited.

This old cross may have been the next cross in line from the Three Stiles Cross, marking the ancient track from Bodmin town south-west to Luxulyan church and beyond to Tywardreath. When first recorded in 1870, the monument had been uprooted from its base-stone and removed to Trevellan Farm within the parish, for use as a simple hedging stone, and built horizontally into the top of a hedge. Here it lay until the 23rd February 1903, when Mr Walter Cock of Trevellan Farm had it re-erected in the grounds of the Mission Chapel at Lockengate. In 1972, the Mission Church was sold and the ancient stone was again moved just a few yards to the crossroads on the A391.

The monument is very roughly hewn and the top of its head has seen considerable damage. The cross displays expanded limbs, formed by four triangular shaped depressions diagonally placed. There are also traces of the narrow bead which once enclosed the head. The cross-shaft appears curved, perhaps reflecting the shape of the piece of stone it was cut from originally; and has a chamfer running down one side.

Height 5ft 3ins (1.6M), width of head 1ft 5ins (0.43M), width of shaft 1ft 1ins (0.33M), thickness 1ft 1ins (0.33M).

Tregonning Cross-head
Luxulyan

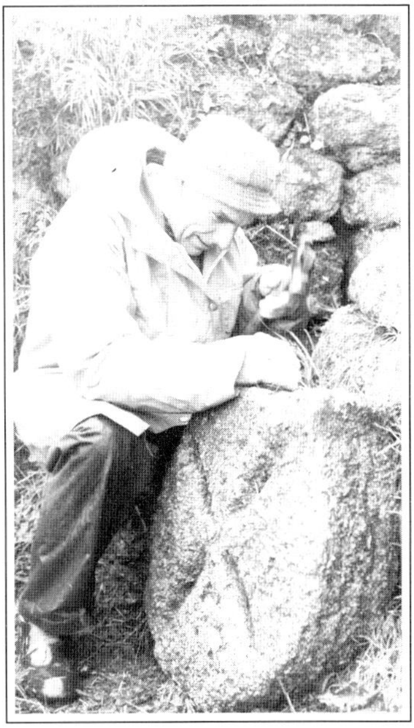

WHEEL-HEADED WAYSIDE CROSS

SX 0539 5702 - Situated 1 mile south of Luxulyan, where the church paths from Methrose and Prideaux meet. Access - Unlimited.

This cross-head was discovered in August 1988 by Mr and Mrs Malcolm Turner of Bodwen, Luxulyan. It was built into the foot of a hedge on the Saints' Way footpath. The following month the author, along with Mr and Mrs Turner, visited the cross site and dug the stone out of the hedge. Sadly, it was found that only the head survived. The site of this discovery was just three yards west of two stiles, where the church path splits, and is likely to have been close to its original position, at the meeting of two ways.

Later, in September 1988, a systematic search for the missing cross-shaft and base-stone was conducted, without success. It was therefore decided by the author and Mr Turner that the cross-head should be erected as near as possible to its site of discovery. Once permission had been granted by the landowners, the author, Mr Turner and Mr Ray Burrows of Bodmin drilled and pinned the cross-head to a large granite stone adjacent to one of the two stiles. The top photograph shows Mr Burrows drilling the cross-head. The work was completed on Saturday 22nd October 1988. Here it can be seen by walkers approaching from either direction along the Saint's Way, which runs from Padstow to Fowey. The cross-head displays a cross in high relief, with widely splayed limbs, enclosed in a narrow bead; the reverse face is similar.

On Ascension day (20th May) 1993, the cross-head was re-dedicated by Captain Robin Grigg of the Church Army, in a ceremony organised by Mrs Constance Rowe and Luxulyan Old Cornwall Society. Today, the site has become overgrown, although the cross-head still marks the route for keen-eyed travellers.

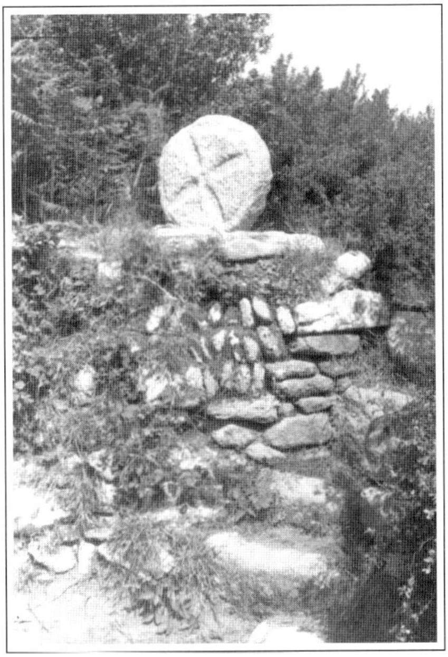

Height of head 1ft 10ins (0.56M), width of head 2ft (0.61M), thickness 7ins (0.18M), probable width of shaft 1ft 4ins (0.405M).

Churchyard Cross
St Mawgan in Pydar

GOTHIC LANTERN CROSS

SW 8722 6594 - Situated on the south-west side of St Mawgan churchyard. St Mawgan lies 3 miles N.W. of St Columb Major. Access - Unlimited.

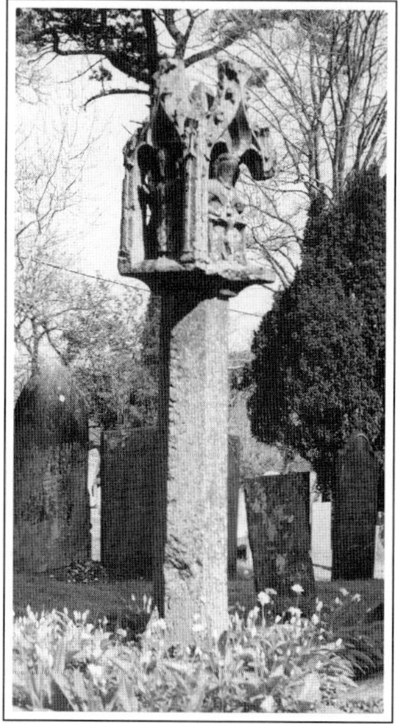

St Mawgan boasts the best preserved medieval lantern cross in the county. The monument is cut from local Cataclewse greenstone and consists of a hexagonal base-stone supporting a hexagonal shaft, which in turn supports the four-sided lantern-style cross-head. It displays ogee arched niches on each face, each containing carved figures. The eastern face displays a representation of the Trinity, with God the Father seated and holding Christ on the Cross. Originally there would have been either a scroll, to represent the Holy Spirit, which would have linked the figures together, or more often an image of a Dove. The western face contains a scene from the Annunciation, the visitation by the Angel Gabriel to the Virgin Mary, with thc news that she would give birth to the Son of God. It shows a representation of the crowned God the Father in the top left hand side of the sculpture, with a ribbon or scroll of the Holy Spirit) issuing from his mouth. The scroll is wrapped around a vase of Lilies (a symbol of purity and the symbol of the Virgin) and the end is held by the Angel Gabriel. To the left, can be seen the Virgin Mary, crowned and standing at a reading desk or *prie-dieu* in a long flowing gown. This stylised scene is

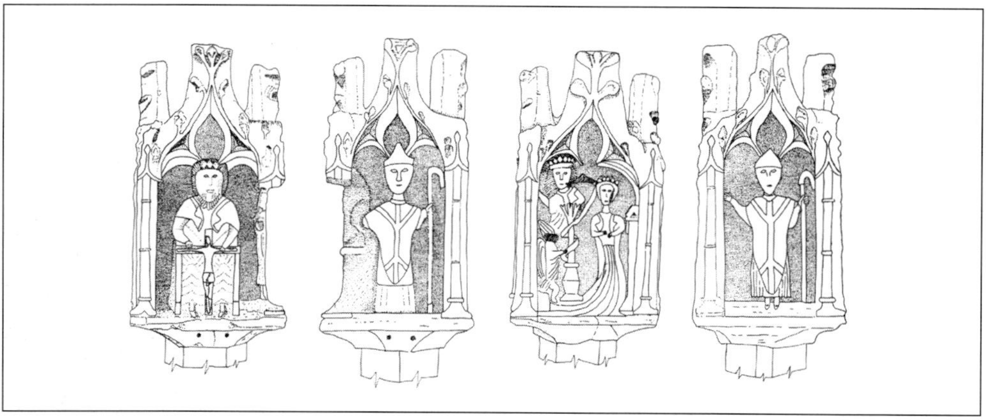

typical of late medieval depictions of the Annunciation. The remaining faces have single figures of bishops wearing chasubles and mitres, and each holding a crosier. The cross is considered to be of late 15th century date and is also thought to be *in situ*.

In 1984, the parochial church council became concerned about the condition of the monument, and sought an estimate to have the cross consolidated for future generations. Over £1,500 was raised by voluntary contributions towards the Lantern Cross appeal. One local student, Simon Harvey, donated all his winnings of £560 from the I.T.V. quiz game 'Connections', towards the appeal. The restoration work was carried out by Oxfordshire craftsman and conservator, Mr Michael Eastham, who began work on the medieval cross in April 1986. Later, on Sunday 29th November 1986, the completed cross was re-dedicated by the Archdeacon of Cornwall, the Venerable Arnold Wood.

Height (complete) 5ft 3ins (1.6M), width of cross-head 1ft 1 1/2ins (0.34M), height of cross-head 2ft (0.61M).

68

Mawgan Cross
St Mawgan in Pydar

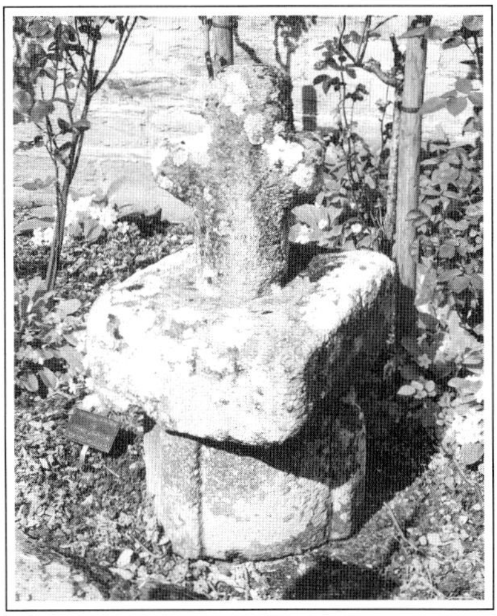

LATIN WAYSIDE CROSS

SW 8725 6595 - Situated below the outside of the chancel wall in the parish churchyard. Access - Unlimited.

The original site of this monument is now in the centre of the main runway of RAF St Mawgan, at SX 8660 6492. The small cross was removed,when the aerodrome was constructed in 1943 by Canon Gunning, rector of St Mawgan, from its site beside a crossroads, to the churchyard where it was set up near the lychgate. The old crossroads was where the St Mawgan churchtown road leading to St Columb Minor was intersected with a road from the hamlet of Trevarrian to St Columb Major. Although the cross may not have been *in situ*, all indications point to the crossroads having been its original site.
The latin cross displays a crudely fashioned relief-carved figure of Christ, consisting of the head and torso with arms outstretched across the horizontal limbs. The lower portion of shaft has long been missing and would have displayed the remaining part of the sculptured figure. The reverse side of the cross-head displays an equal-limbed cross in relief, and was formerly whitewashed; the shaft is unornamented. There is no record of when the monument was originally damaged. In 1974, the cross was again resited from the lychgate to its present position below the chancel window.

Height 1ft 5ins (0.43M), width of head 12 1/2ins (0.32M), thickness 8ins (0.2M), base 1ft 6ins square (0.455M) height 9ins (0.23M).

69

Bodrean Cross
St Mawgan in Pydar

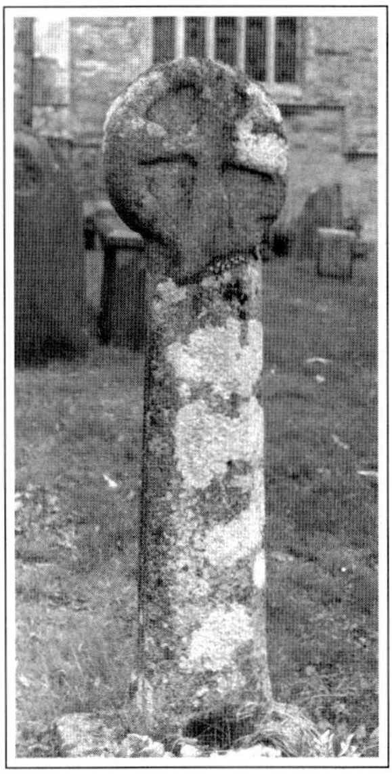

WHEEL-HEADED WAYSIDE CROSS

SW 8725 6594 - On the south side of St Mawgan in Pydar churchyard, amongst the tombstones. Access - Unlimited.

In 1904, this small wheel-headed cross, with a fragment of shaft attached was discovered in an old pigsty at Bodrean Farm (SW 8484 4790) in the parish of St. Clement. The monument was later rescued and removed to St Mawgan in Pydar churchyard in 1906 by A.C.P. Williams Esq. of Bodrean; the Williamses of Bodrean being a branch of the same family which formerly owned Carnanton Estate at St Mawgan. Here, the cross-head of Cateclewse stone was set up on a modern chamfered shaft with a base-stone cut from fine-grained granite, and utilised as a private gravestone to the Rev J. O. Gunning, rector of St Mawgan from 1927 to 1946, and his wife.
The cross-head displays an equal-limbed cross in relief with expanded ends formed by four triangular depressions and is probably of late medieval date. Sadly, the mixture of granite and Cateclewse is unsatisfactory, although the proportions of the restored monument are good.

Cross-head height 1ft 2ins (0.355M), width 1ft 1ins (0.33M), thickness 6ins (0.15M), total height 4ft 8 1/2ins (1.435M).

Lanherne Cross
St Mawgan in Pydar

FOUR-HOLED MEMORIAL or PREACHING CROSS

SW 8723 6591 - Situated in the grounds of Lanherne convent, close to the entrance to the public chapel. Access - Unlimited.

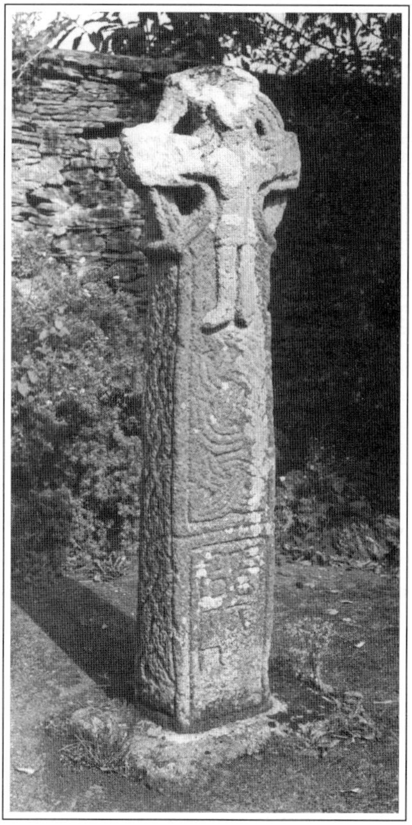

In 1993, the County Record Office acquired a collection of documents relating to the Arundell family. Within this collection, known as the Arundell archive, was a watercolour sketch of this beautiful cross. It consists of a crude drawing of both faces of the monument with the following inscription, dated 1777 - *'An inscription on the fore and back part of a Cross lying amongst the ruins of an Antient Chapel in a field called the Chapel Close, parcel of the Farm or Barton of Roseworthy in Cornwall, Belonging to the right honoble Lord Arundell'.* From this we can assume that the monument was no longer revered as it was lying down in the ruins of the chapel, although the fact that someone in 1777 considered in worth recording, may have led to its eventual rescue and removal. It is not known exactly when the cross was removed from Roseworthy in Gwinear to its present site in the grounds of Lanherne. The Lyson brothers recorded the cross in its present position in 1814, and so it is possible that it had been removed to Lanherne. In 1794, the ancient mansion house was made into a refuge for nuns of the Carmelite Order, who had fled from Antwerp, Belgium, when the French Revolutionary armies laid seige to the city. Perhaps the cross was an additional gift to this religious order.

The elaborate decoration on this monument is a great credit to the craftsman, who chose Pentewan stone rather than granite, enabling intricate patterns to be adopted. The four-holed cross encapsulates several forms of ornamentation, consisting of a figure depicting the Crucifixion on the front of the cross-head, with a triple-beaded figure-of-eight knotwork in a large panel below and an inscription in Hiberno Saxon characters enclosed in another panel below this. The inscription reads *+BrE IDEᴛI mA h* in four horizontal lines which translated by Iago reads, *'The Blessed Eid and Imah'.*

The reverse face displays five bosses, one in the centre of the cross-head, with another on each of the four limbs of the cross. These bosses are said to represent the five wounds that Christ received at the Crucifixion. Below this is more triple-beaded knotwork with a second inscription in a small panel near the base of the shaft, which reads *ruhol.* A similar name *runho* appears on a churchyard cross at Sancreed, and it has been suggested that the two monuments may have been cut by the same craftsman, or commissioned by the same man - Ruhol. The remaining sides display interlace work and the unusual zoomorphic interlace decoration which can also be seen on the Sancreed cross: a serpent-type beast, with its head at the bottom of the shaft and body interlaced.

Height 4ft 10 1/2ins (1.485M), width of head 1ft 4 1/2ins (0.42M), width of shaft (at neck) 9 1/2ins (0.24M), width of shaft (at base) 11 1/2ins (0.29M), thickness 6 1/2ins to 8ins (0.15M to 0.2M).

71

Tresillian Cross
Merther

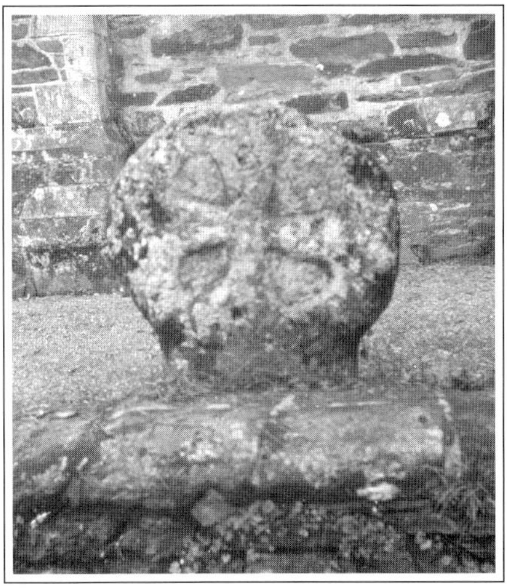

WHEEL-HEADED WAYSIDE CROSS

SW 8702 4648 - Outside the western side of the Holy Trinity Church at Tresillian. Tresillian village lies 3 1/2 miles N.E. of the City of Truro. Access - Unlimited.

This cross-head, with a short portion of shaft, was discovered at a site known as 'Chapel Field', at Tregellas, 1 1/2 miles north-east of Probus churchtown. In 1863 it was removed for preservation to the mission churchyard at Tresillian in the neighbouring parish of Merther by Captain Pinwell of Trehane at Probus, and erected on the church wall. When the cross was removed to the churchyard it was supported by half of a large base-stone. In 1904, when a new church was built, incorporating part of the former mission church, the base-stone disappeared, although the cross remains.

The monument displays an equal-limbed cross, formed by four triangular depressions, similar in style to the Trevellan Cross at Lockengate, Luxulyan (no 65 in this guide). There is no knowledge of the cross-shaft which may well be in use as a gatepost near its former site, and it is also not known whether the half base-stone was removed from Tregellas, or where it went when the present church was built. The monument probably marked a route to the ancient chapel at Tregellas, of which no remains exist today.

Height 2ft 1ins (0.635M), width of head 2ft 1 1/2ins (0.645M), width of shaft 1ft 4ins (0.405M), thickness varies from 5ins to 9ins (0.127M to 0.228M).

72

Fentongollan Cross
St Michael Penkivel

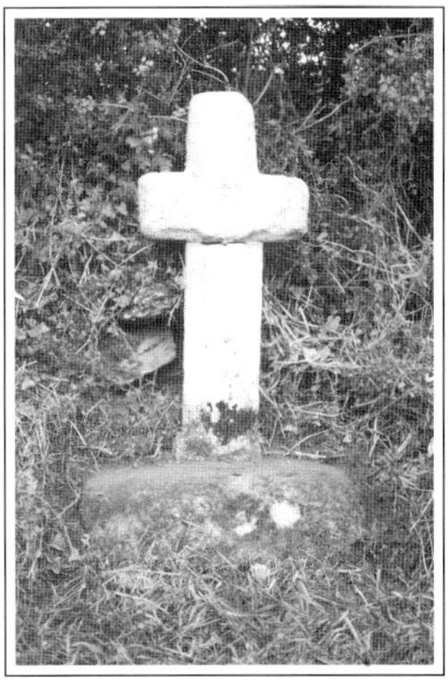

GOTHIC LATIN CROSS

SW 8556 4272 - Situated a 1/4 mile north-west of St Michael Penkivel Church. Access - Unlimited.

This is one of two Gothic latin crosses recorded in the parish of St Michael Penkivel (sometimes spelt Penkevil). The second cross was removed to Canada by the Rev F. L. Osler prior to 1880, (see chapter on 'Crosses in Exile'), but this particular monument still stands beside the road from Tresillian to St Michael's church at a junction with a lane leading down to Malpas Point. Only the upper and horizontal limbs of the cross-head are original; these have chamfered angles, giving an octagonal section. The monument was restored using an old window mullion for its shaft. The base stone also appears to be relatively modern and definitely not of the correct style to support this type of cross.

The cross may be connected with the site of an old graveyard, holy well and ancient chapel just to the north. The field directly behind the cross is still known as 'Cross Meadow'.

Height 1ft 4ins (0.405M), width of head 1ft 6ins (0.46M), thickness 6 1/2ins (0.165M), total height of restored cross 4ft 3ins (1.295M).

73

Church porch Cross-base
St Michael Penkivel

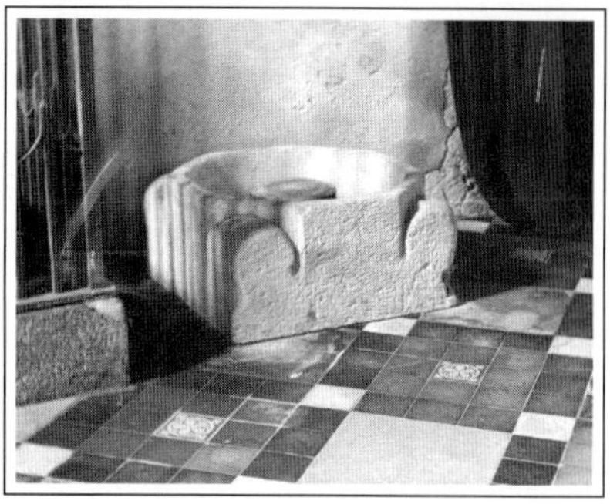

GOTHIC CROSS-BASE

SW 8578 4215 - Situated in the south porch of the parish church. Access - when the porch door is unlocked, normally during daylight hours.

This base of Pentewan stone lies protected from the weather inside the church porch. The general appearance of the stone suggests that the mortice was at some time hollowed out to its limit, and utilised as a container for shrubs or plants. A hole has been cut through the bottom of this stone, presumably for drainage, which gives some credence to this assumption. The base-stone may have originally supported a churchyard cross, of which no remains exist. A similar base-stone of Gothic date at West Pentire in the parish of Crantock, is still in use as a plant holder.

Height 1ft (0.305M), width 2 ft. sq. (0.61M).

74a

Churchyard Cross
Newlyn East

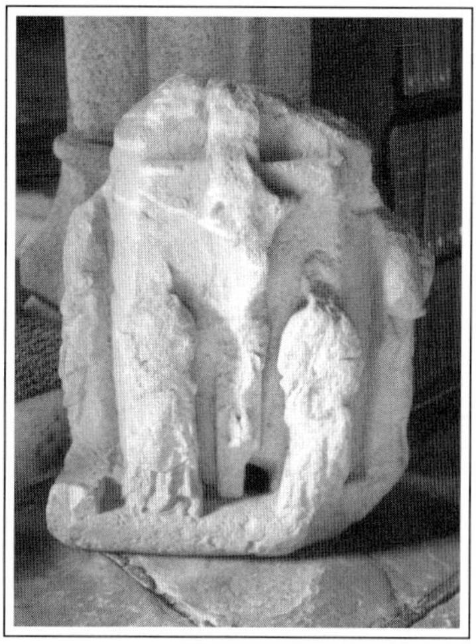

GOTHIC LANTERN CROSS

SW 8288 5633 - Leaning against a column inside the parish church, near the font. Access - only when the church is unlocked.

This badly mutilated lantern cross is cut from a grey elvan. It features a scene from the Crucifixion on its front face, depicting Christ on the cross with two witnesses, possibly Mary the mother of Jesus and St John. The reverse face depicts the mutilated remains of a sculptured figure of the Virgin Mary and Child, while the remaining faces of the monument display single figures, one of whom is probably St Newlyn, carrying her severed head.

The stone was discovered in 1959, buried in the churchyard. It is therefore interesting to find that the great Cornish historian, William Borlase, described a similar stone in both sculpture and dimensions at Treledra (Treluddra) Farm between the years 1751 and 1755. Borlase recorded, *'...call'd in at Treluddra nothing of antiquity worth notice there but a stone carved like a pedestal with a square socket on the top of it as if to receive either a statue or a cross - it was hollowed and pierced quite through. On the front of it in a nitch was our Saviour on the Cross - a thief on each hand. In each of the other three fronts was a single image I suppose the Virgin Mother, St John and the other Mary. I had not time to draw this stone which is about 2 feet high'.*

This description differs somewhat from what one can see today, and it is unfortunate that Borlase did not have more time to examine the stone and present a better description. In the author's opinion it is probably the same monument, although today there is no evidence of any square socket. His description of the figures is similar, even though he interprets the scenes differently. It is now unlikely that we will ever know if the two monument were the same, and if so, when the lantern cross was removed to the churchyard, and why it became lost and subsquently buried in the churchyard.

Height 1ft 9ins (0.535M), width 1ft 5ins(0.43M), thickness 9ins (0.23M).

74b

Base of Churchyard cross Newlyn East

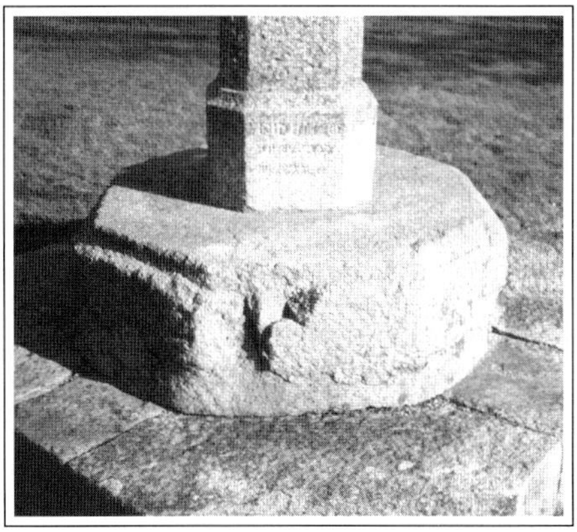

GOTHIC CROSS-BASE

SW 8286 5634 - Situated on the western side of the churchyard. Access - Unlimited.

A memorial cross, which stands near the western entrance to the churchyard, was erected in 1880 in memory of parishioners who died in a cholera epidemic. It displays what appears to be a medieval cross-base. The composite monument consists of an octagonal platform, made from cut granite blocks, which in turn supports the medieval octagonal cross-base, which holds a modern gothic-style latin cross. The cross is more reminiscent of a Dartmoor or Devonshire monument.

Baird suggested that the old base-stone was brought to the churchyard from Trehane, a quarter of a mile to the west of the church, although he does not give any reason for this. Furthermore, the street running due west from the church is known as 'The Cross', and although the site of a crossroads in the village, it is also suggestive of either a village or market cross.

Diameter 3ft 8ins (1.12M), height 1ft 2ins (0.355M).

75

Neeham Cross-base Newlyn East

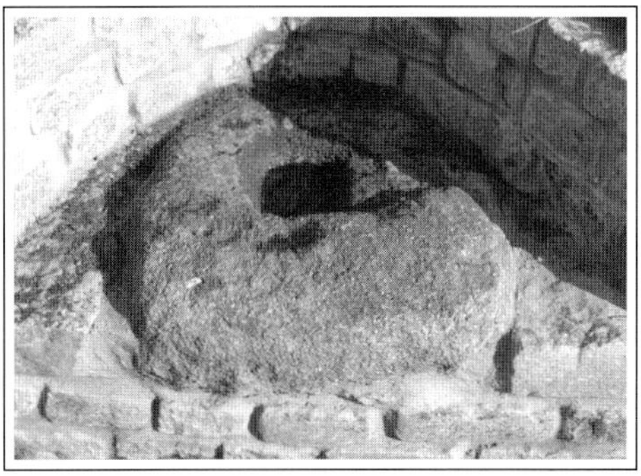

WAYSIDE CROSS-BASE

SW 8266 5656 - Situated 1/4 mile north-west of the parish church on Neeham Road, which leads to Tregear. Access - Unlimited.

The churchtown of Newlyn East has roads and tracks radiating out from it in all directions; most of these would have originally been single pack horse tracks or footpaths. The only one to survive as a footpath now leads from the church, in a north-west direction, and today acts as a short cut to Neeham Road and on towards Tregear. (Tregair), bypassing the main village. Lying beside the road at the point where the path meets the road, is the base of a wayside cross, probably *in situ*. In recent years the cross-base has been protected by cut granite stones cemented in place, forming a small recess in the hedge.

Although there are no wayside crosses recorded in Newlyn East, documentary evidence and field names suggest that at one time several may have existed. No less than fifteen fields recorded in the Tithe Apportionment map of 1840 have the name Cross written in either English or Cornish; such as Cross Close, *Park an Groweth* etc.

Recently, the parish council has gained Scheduled Monument Consent to erect a new granite wayside cross in the cross-base. The project is being organised by Councillor Mrs M. Callis. The author has supplied a design for the cross, which is to be carved by Mr Harold Phillips of Constantine, with granite supplied by Mr John Olds, also of Constantine. The cross-base was formerly recorded as the Tregear cross-base. See page no 85 for last minute developments.

Width 2ft 6ins (0.76M) by 2ft 3ins (0.685M), thickness 8ins (0.2M), mortice 9ins (0.23M) by 6 1/2ins (0.165M), depth 5ins (0.125M).

St Piran's Cross, Perranzabuloe

PREACHING or BOUNDARY CROSS

SW 7720 5646 - Situated on Penhale Sands, 1 1/2 miles SW of Cubert church and 2 3/4 miles NE of Perranporth. Access - Unlimited, there is a public right of way to the cross.

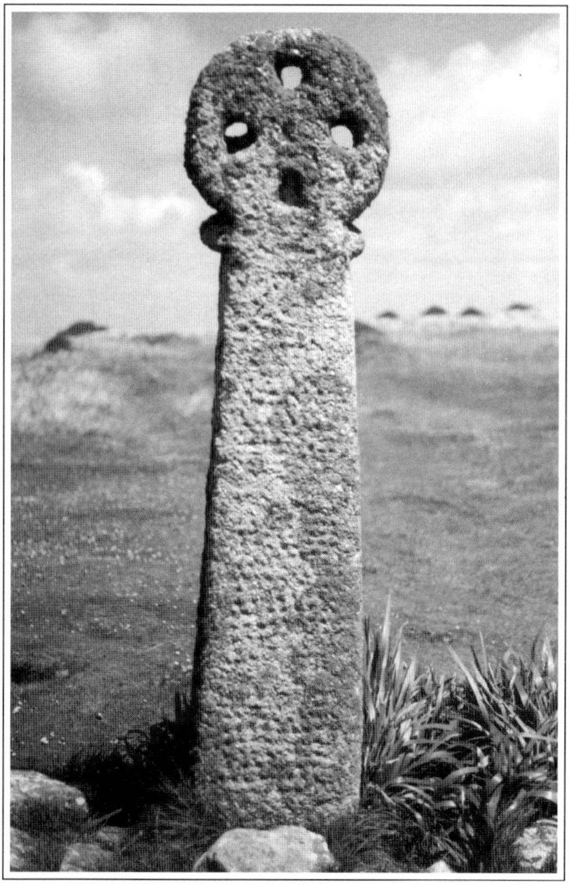

This cross stands amongst sandhills, half a mile east of St Piran's first church or oratory, (which was reburied in the sand in 1980) and immediately south of the ruins of St Piran's second church. This second church was the parish church until 1805 and the cross stands within its original churchyard. Both the oratory chapel and parish church were abandoned due to encroaching sand and flooding and led to the present church being built, inland at Lambourne.

The cross is claimed to be the *Cristelmael,* recorded as part of the boundary of the large manor of Tywarnhayle, in a charter dated 960AD, during the reign of King Edgar, and if it is referring to the cross, would be the earliest reference to a stone cross in Cornwall. According to Henderson, the *Cristelmael* means 'Christmound' or crucifix and he suggests that the word must have a close connection with the church or the cross. In 1617, the chancel of the parish church is named as the actual boundary of the manor.

The massive four-holed granite cross has its holes cut in the vertical and horizontal positions, forming a diagonal or St Andrew's Cross; the lower hole is only pierced part way through the stone. It also displays a central boss on each face. The stone is cut from coarse-grained granite and has small projections at the neck. The monument is decorated with punch-dots placed in tight horizontal lines, and this appears to be the only form of decoration on all four sides of the monument, although further decoration may have been lost through hundreds of years of blowing sand. In his publication, *Old Cornish Crosses*, Langdon illustrated a base-stone, which today is not visible, and noted the height as eight feet ten inches. Today the ground level is considerably higher, due to shifting sands, and the height of the cross has been reduced to seven feet four inches. The monument is similar in style to the Three Hole Cross in the parish of Egloshayle (North Cornwall no 32).

Height 7ft4ins (2.24M), width of head 2ft (0.61M), width of shaft (at neck) 1ft 2ins (0.355M), width of shaft (at ground level) 1ft 6 1/2ins (0.47M), thickness varies between 11ins to 14ins (0.28M to 0.355M).

77

Nansmellyn Cross
Perranzabuloe

BOUNDARY CROSS or BOUND STONE

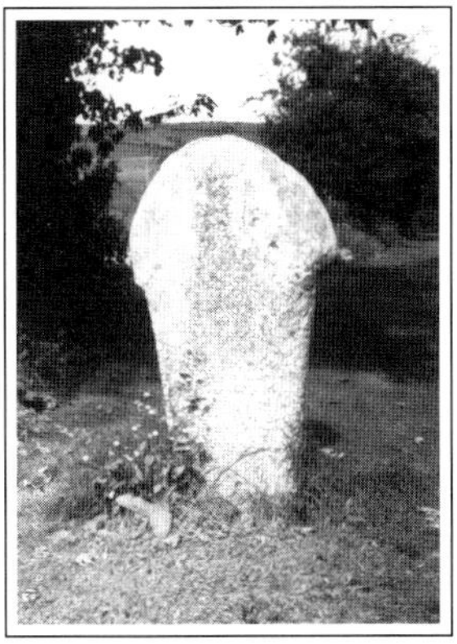

SW 7811 5319 - On the driveway to Silver Bow Caravan Park beside the A3075 Redruth to Newquay road. Access - The stone is on private property, although a public right of way exists.

The author has decided to include this boundary stone, although it is not strictly a cross, because it has often been referred to as a cross. It was first recorded as a cross in 1896, by Langdon in his publication, *Old Cornish Crosses* and according to him had been re-used as a boundstone. The monument was first recorded as a boundstone in 1587, marking the boundary of Carnkief. Langdon also recorded that the stone was near the site of St Piran's Well, and had displayed on one shoulder an inscription, which read NANS-MEE-LYN, in three horizontal lines. The inscription is only lightly incised, and suggests that it was at some time adopted as a boundary stone for the manor of Nansmellyn. The author suggests that if it was originally designed as a boundary stone for this manor, the inscription would have been much bolder and probably in a more prominent position on the monument. It is difficult to decide what distance was implied by 'near', as today the stone is situated almost half a mile from the well site, and therefore one is unable to decide whether the stone has been moved, or not.
No sign of a cross symbol exists on either face of the stone, which although rounded is by no means a wheel-headed cross. Henderson also noted the stone as a defaced cross, although there is no evidence to suggest it has been re-cut. There are similar boundary stones in the parishes of Madron, St Columb Minor and Colan.

Height 3ft 4ins (1.105M), width of head 1ft 10ins (0.56M), width of shaft (at neck) 1ft 5 1/2ins (0.445M), width of shaft (at ground) 1ft 1 1/2ins (0.34M), thickness 8ins (0.2M).

78

St Piran's Oratory Cross, Perranzabuloe

GABLE CROSS

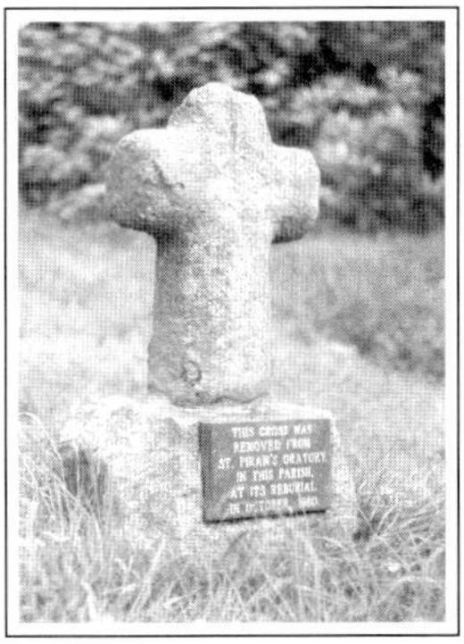

SX 7706 5204 - Situated on the south side of Perranzabuloe parish church at Lambourne, 2 miles S E of Perranporth. Access - Unlimited.

It is not known from where this small gable cross came from originally, but for many years it stood fixed to the gable end of the concrete shelter protecting the ruins of St Piran's Oratory, 1/2 mile west of St Piran's four-holed cross (no 76 in this guide). In 1980, after many years of discussion about the plight of the Oratory, it was decided to demolish the shelter and rebury the ruins, until a better form of preservation from flooding and sand encroachment was possible. It was at this time that the small cross was taken down and removed to the modern parish churchyard at Lambourne, where it was mounted on a granite pedestal with a suitable plaque. The plaque reads *'This cross was removed from St Piran's Oratory in this parish at its reburial in October 1980'.* In the author's opinion the weathered cross appears to have originally been octagonal in section, suggesting a date much later than the Oratory building. The stone may perhaps have been removed from the old parish church near St Piran's cross, which was excavated between the years 1917 and 1919, soon after the concrete shelter had been erected over the building (built 1910).

Height 1ft 10ins (0.56M), width of shaft 8ins (0.2M), width of head 1ft 4 1/2ins (0.42M), thickness 5 1/2ins to 6 1/2ins (0.14M to 0.19M).

79

Trelowthas Cross, Probus

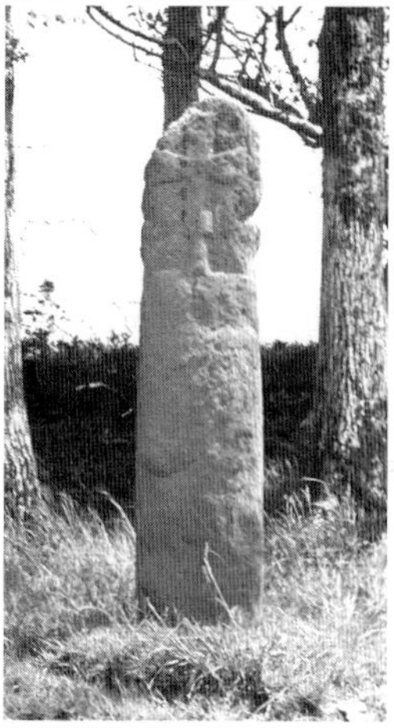

WHEEL-HEADED WAYSIDE or BOUNDARY CROSS

SW 8857 4666 - Situated at the entrance to Trelowthas Farm, 1 1/2 miles south-west of Probus churchtown. Access - Although the cross is on private ground, it is situated beside a public right of way, which also acts as the farm drive.

This cross was discovered by Mr William Moyle in the 1940s, covering a well in the grounds of Trelowthas. The cross was originally round-headed, although much of the head has been chipped away in the past. It is cut from a piece of fine blue elvan, which on first examination appears to be slate. On both faces are carved latin crosses in relief, with expanded ends to their limbs. On one face, the lower limb of the cross is extended part way down the cross-shaft and at the neck of the shaft there are the characteristic projections seen on many of the North Cornwall crosses. Henderson recorded eleven ancient chapels in the parish of Probus, one of which was situated at Great Trelowthas and was licensed in May 1379. The parish was also one of four in the county to have the privilege of a Sanctuary, which extended beyond the four walls of the church, (the others being at Padstow, St Keverne and St Buryan). The boundary was said to extend to the east as far as the Carvossa Cross, which is missing, and considering that the Trelowthas cross is at equal distance on the west side of Probus church, it seems possible that this cross marked the western boundary of the Sanctuary. Mr William Moyle was made a Bard of the Cornish Gorsedd in 1949 for his services to Cornish history, and took the Bardic name: *Dyscudhor Crowsow* (Finder of Crosses).

Height 4ft 6ins (1.37M), width of head 1ft 1ins (0.33M), width of shaft 1ft 1 1/2ins (0.345M), thickness 4 1/2ins (0.115M).

80

Churchyard Cross, Roche

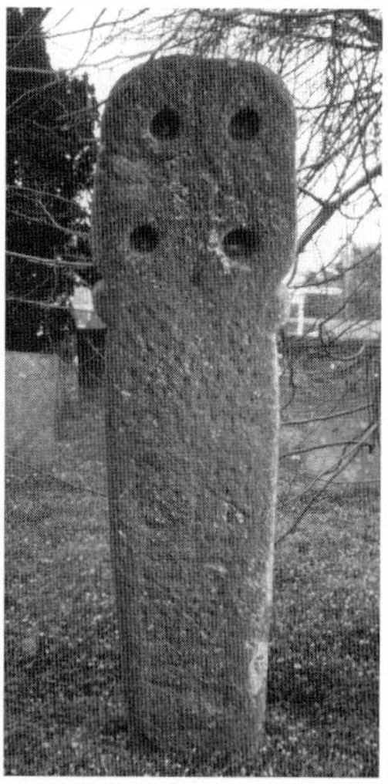

WHEEL-HEADED CHURCHYARD CROSS

SW 9879 5978 - Situated on the south side of the parish churchyard. Roche is 6 miles north of St Austell. Access - Unlimited.

This massive monolith of moorland granite stands *in situ* on the south side of the churchyard. The cross-head displays four irregular circular depressions, the centres of which are slightly raised. A boss with an enclosed bead around it is positioned between the lower two circular depressions, rather than being set centrally on the cross-head between the four. The reverse face is similar, but shows a centrally positioned boss. Although the stone is classed as a wheel-headed cross, the head is in fact almost square, with rounded corners. At the neck of the monument are projections on each side and the shaft has a pronounced entasis. The shaft, on both sides, is decorated with groups of small holes in a crude form with incised lines separating the groups. On one edge of the shaft the stone is beaded with short horizontal beads between forming a ribbed effect. On the remaining edge there are more small holes along with three small incised circles and the most unusual symbol to be found on a Cornish cross, which is a sword, complete with hilt. Today, the ground level has risen by two and a half feet due to interments, and the base-stone is now concealed from sight. The only similar monument is in the old graveyard at Merther Uny in Wendron parish, although it is very much smaller.

Height 6ft 2ins (1.88M), width of head 2ft 2ins (0.66M), width of shaft (at neck) 1ft 9ins (0.535M), width of shaft (at ground level) 1ft 6ins (0.455M), thickness 12ins to 14ins (0.305M to 0.355M).

81

Glebe Cross
Roche

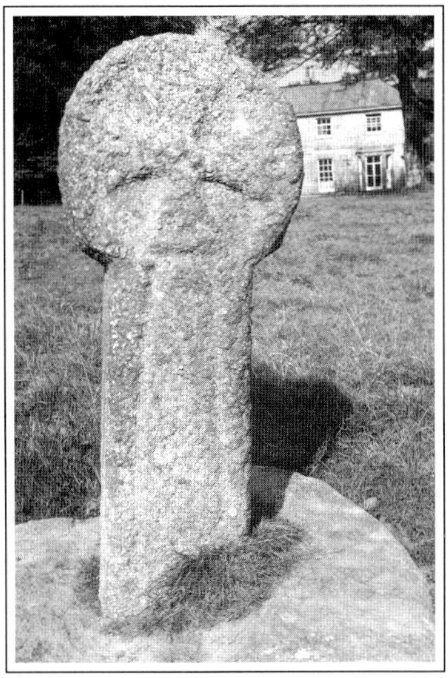

WHEEL-HEADED WAYSIDE CROSS

SW 9876 5990 - Situated in the field on the eastern side of the churchyard. Access - The field where the cross stands is private, but the stone can be viewed from the roadside.

Now standing near the centre of the rectory meadow, it is uncertain whether this cross is in its original position. Polsue stated that the monument was removed there for preservation, while Langdon considered it to be *in situ*. The true facts about this monument's original position will probably never be proved unless earlier documentary evidence is discovered. The head displays an equal-limbed cross with expanded ends, formed by four triangular depressions, and a small hole at the centre. The reverse face is similar, but more pronounced, and the limbs appear to be slightly crooked when compared to the front face. The shaft of the monument is plain, except for a narrow bead running down each edge.

Height 4ft (1.22M), width of shaft 1ft 2ins (0.355M), thickness 7ins to 9ins (0.18M to 0.23M), width of head 1ft 10ins(0.56M).

82

Trerank Cross
Roche

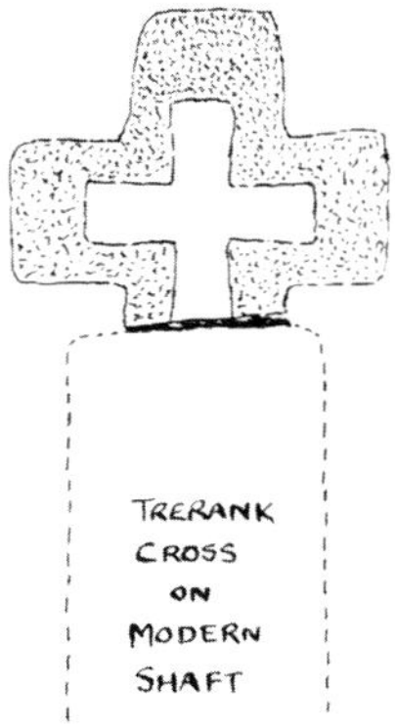

LATIN WAYSIDE CROSS-HEAD

SW 9869 6002 - Situated in the garden of the old rectory at Roche. Access - The cross stands in private grounds, there is no public access.

It is interesting to note that all three of Roche's crosses are completely different in both design and date. The Trerank cross-head was discovered in 1902 by Mr Dempster, the local schoolmaster, built into a hedge on Trerank Lane, which leads from the church south-west to Trerank Farm. Here the stone remained until 1921 when it was rescued by the Rev E. A. Lowe, rector of Roche church, and removed to the rectory gardens for preservation.

The latin cross-head consists of the upper and horizontal limbs with a small fragment of its shaft. The front of the cross-head has a second latin cross in relief carved upon it, although the reverse face remains plain. Mr Cresswell Payne, a local historian of Roche, suggested that the stone may have been a gable cross or finial, although the author considers from its size that it was originally a free standing monument. A search of the gateposts and stiles in the Trerank area could prove this, if the missing shaft was discovered. Today, the Old Rectory is a private residence, and the cross is supported by a modern granite pillar beside the house. There are crosses of similar style (i.e. a latin cross with a second latin cross superimposed in relief upon the head) at St Cleer holy well (East Cornwall no 39), Triffle, St Germans (East Cornwall no 47) and also in the churchyard at Tresmeer (North Cornwall no 99).

Height of cross-head 1ft 6ins (0.46M), width of cross-head 1ft 10ins (0.56M), thickness 7ins (0.178M).

83

Old Rectory Cross
Ruan Lanihorne

GOTHIC LATIN CROSS

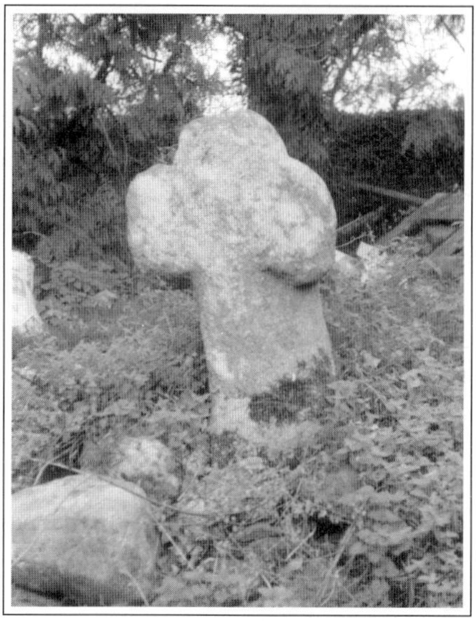

SW 8957 4223 - Situated in the grounds of the old rectory, just north of the village. Ruan Lanihorne is 2 1/2 miles S.W. of Tregony. Access - The cross stands in private grounds; there is no public access.

Discovered prior to 1920, buried in the parish churchyard, this granite cross was later removed to the grounds of the new rectory and set up at the end of the drive, close to the house. The small cross was originally octagonal in section, although today, due to many years of weathering its section is almost round. The cross has short stunted limbs, the upper one of which has been fractured, and there is no evidence to suggest that the shaft was ever any longer. The monument is now cemented to a second piece of shaft.
In the author's opinion the stone was formerly a gable cross or finial from the church. Since the first edition of this guide, the Old Rectory has changed ownership at least twice and the author is unable to ascertain whether the monument is still there.

Height 1ft 8ins (0.51M), width of head 1ft 2 1/2ins (0.37M), width of shaft 7 3/4ins (0.195M), Thickness 6ins (0.15M).

84

Churchyard Cross
St Stephen in Brannel

GOTHIC CHURCHYARD CROSS

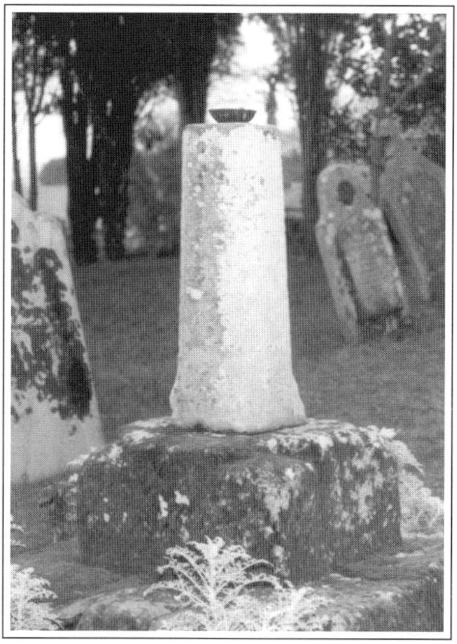

SW 9450 5329 - Situated on the south side of the parish churchyard, St Stephen in Brannel lies 5 miles west of St Austell. Access - Unlimited.

The cross-shaft and pedestal is all that remains of this Gothic churchyard cross, the head of which may have been of the lantern type. The octagonal shaft of Pentewan stone features chamfer stops at the bottom and is mortice-jointed into a pedestal of similar material, which in turn is supported by a lower base formed with blocks of Pentewan stone. Originally, the cross-shaft would have been much higher, and today only this short portion exists.
St Stephen in Brannel, until the 19th century, was the mother church for St Dennis and Caerhays and today its parish stands on the southern side of the main china clay area.

Height of shaft 2ft 7 3/4ins (0.805M), pedestal 2ft 2ins square (0.66M), pedestal height 1ft 2ins (0.355M).

85

Treneague Cross
St Stephen in Brannel

WHEEL-HEADED WAYSIDE CROSS

SW 9450 5329 - Situated on the south side of the parish churchyard. Access - Unlimited.

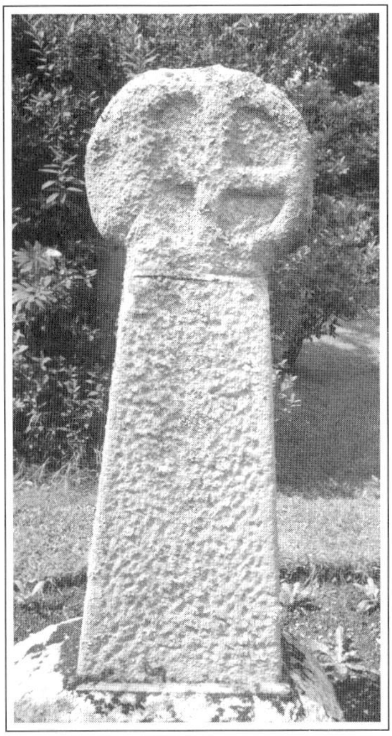

Found at the end of the nineteenth century in a field on Treneague Farm, the cross-head was later removed to the churchyard and re-erected on a modern shaft and base-stone. Treneague is 1/2 mile north-west of the churchtown, and is on the direct route with the old church path leading to Trethosa.

There is very little information regarding the discovery of this old stone. Langdon recorded its existence but did not actually view the monument. The cross was probably erected as a wayside cross marking the path towards the church, although Treneague also once had an ancient chapel, which according to records was licenced in 1381; this may have been a further reason for erecting the cross.

The main face of the granite round-headed stone displays an equal-limbed cross in relief with parallel limbs, which have been formed by cutting four triangular depressions; the reverse face features a similar cross. The upper segment of the cross is badly chipped on the front. Only 1 1/2ins of the original shaft survives; the remainder might be holding up a gate somewhere in the parish, or acting as a lintel in a nearby building.

Height of cross-head 1ft 6 3/4ins (0.475M), width 1ft 9ins (0.53M), thickness 5ins (0.125M).

86A

St Dominic Street Cross-head
St Mary's Truro

GOTHIC LATIN CROSS-HEAD

At present the cross-head is in storage at the County Museum in River Street, Truro, and is not on public view.

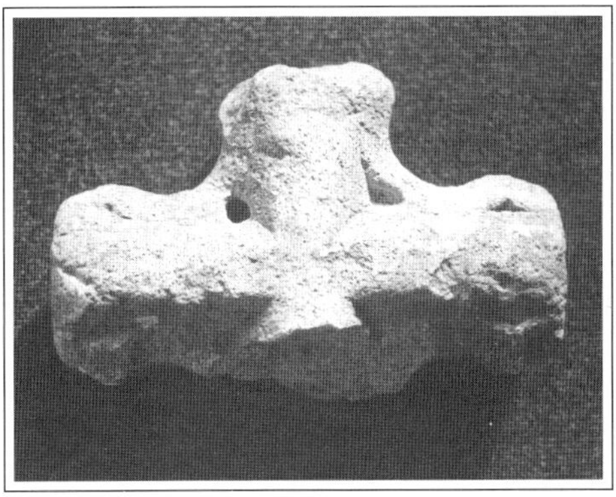

This small cross-head, carved from Pentewan stone, was discovered in 1976, during building work in the back yard of no 23 St Dominic Street in Truro. The stone displays chamfered angles and cusps between the cross-limbs and is exceptionally well executed. It is similar in style to, but smaller than, the Tresallyn Cross at St Merryn (see North Cornwall no 78), although the Tresallyn Cross is carved from Cateclewse greenstone.

One can assume from the size of the cross-head that it was originally a gable cross, which may have once adorned the gable of an ancient eccelesiatical building, probably the church of the the Dominican Friary, which once graced Truro and gives its name to St Dominic Street.

Height 8 1/4ins (0.21M), width of head 1ft (0.305M) thickness 3 1/2ins (0.09M).

High Cross
St Mary's Truro

WHEEL-HEADED WAYSIDE CROSS

SW 8256 4490 - Stands on the west side of the Cathedral, close to the Post Office. Access - Unlimited.

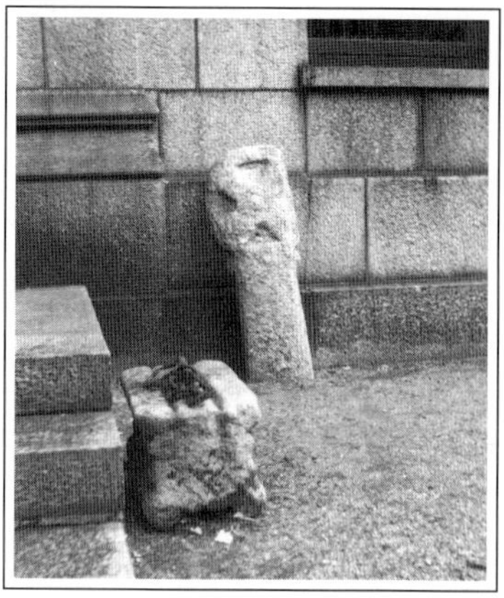

The area directly west of St Mary's church, now incorporated into Truro's Cathedral, has been known for many centuries as 'the cross' or 'High Cross'. In a document dated 1290, there is reference to a stone cross in Truro (*crucem lapideam burgi de Truru)* and later in 1755, when the old bull ring was removed, it was suggested by Henderson that the bulls may have been baited to the base-stone of this cross.

In 1958, while a deep trench was being excavated in St Nicholas Street, the upper section of a stone cross was discovered and rescued by Mr H.L. Douch, the former Curator of the Museum in River Street. The workmen digging the trench stated that a similar portion of granite stone was also found, but had been reburied in the trench further along the road. This was presumably the lower part of the cross-shaft.

The cross was left outside the Museum (see photograph above) until 1959, when it was erected in a flower border against the western wall of the Cathedral. There it stood until December 1981; but in that year the monument was repositioned outside Marks and Spencer's store when the area was being cobbled. In this new position the ancient stone could be examined from both sides, but was unfortunately not respected by many passers-by, being sometimes used as a leaning post, or a prop for market stalls. This concerned Truro City Councillor John Christie, so much that he began a campaign for the stone to be lengthened and converted into a proper 'High' cross.

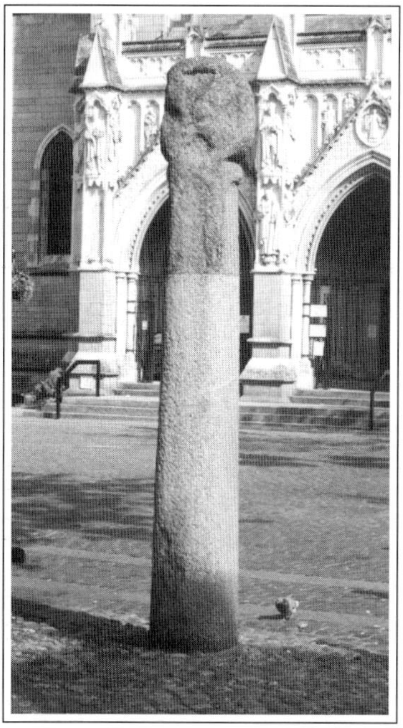

After obtaining financial assistance from various bodies, Mr Christie accepted a quotation from Hantergantick granite quarry to extend the cross shaft by six feet and the monument was removed to the quarry at St Breward in April 1987. Here, stonemason Mr Peter Nottle undertook the task of sawing and cutting the new shaft, which was pinned and glued to the existing cross. Later, in March 1988, the cross was finally completed and re-erected at its former site at High Cross. To mark the end of Councillor Christie's year of office as the Mayor of Truro, he arranged for the High Cross to be re-dedicated. This ceremony was conducted by the Dean of Truro, the Very Rev. David Shearlock, during Evensong on the 10th May 1992.

In the author's opinion, the original High Cross at Truro was more likely to have been a gothic monument, a latin cross on a stepped base, whereas this cross has all the hall-marks of a typical wayside cross.

Height prior to restoration 3ft 11ins (1.195M), height after restoration 10ft (3.05M), width of head 1ft 7ins (0.48M), width of shaft 11 1/2ins to 13 1/2ins (0.29M to 0.34M), thickness 11ins to 12ins (0.28M to 0.305M).

87

Tretherras Reliquary Cross-head St Mary's Truro

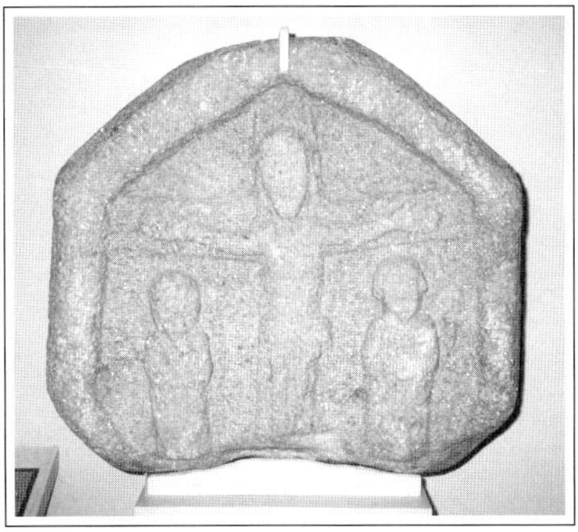

LANTERN CROSS/RELIQUARY

SW 8235 4489 - In the County Museum at River Street, Truro. Access - The Museum is open to the public Monday to Saturday. There is an admission charge. There is no free admission to view the stone only.

Tretherras Farm lies 1/4 mile south of St Allen churchtown. This small triangular shaped stone, with hollowed out back and a sculptured scene of the Crucifixion, was discovered amongst other carved stones at the farm. These carved stones were removed from the ruins of an ancient chapel of St Martin, which stood in a field between Lanner and Tretherras. When the stone was seen by Mary Henderson in 1958, it was in use as a trough for chicken feed. When the farm was sold in 1972, the stone was acquired by a Mr Carveth of Truro, who later presented it to the Royal Institution of Cornwall Museum in Truro. Here the stone is on display in the main exhibition hall and is labelled as a Gothic lantern cross. Despite this it has been suggested that the stone was never a cross but was a reliquary or altar piece, where holy relics would have been placed. In support of this theory are similar stones in Breage church and St Petroc's, Bodmin, where the front face depicts scenes from the Crucifixion, with its back hollowed out to receive relics.

Height 1ft 4ins (0.405M), width 1ft 4 1/2ins (0.42M), thickness 10ins (0.255M).

88

Cross-shaft in Churchyard Tywardreath

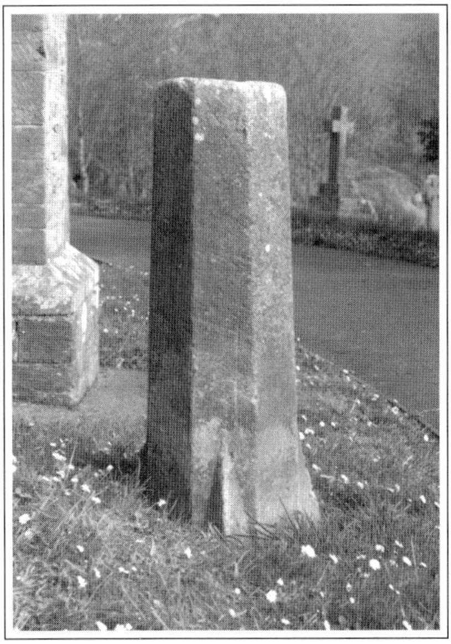

GOTHIC CROSS-SHAFT

SX 0848 5429 - Close to the south porch of St Andrew's parish church, Tywardreath. Access - Unlimited.

This portion of octagonal cross-shaft, which is cut from fine grained granite, was first noted by Langdon in 1896 as being near Par railway station. Later, in the 1920s, a stone answering to the same description was recorded at St Andrew's bridge, which is only a few hundred yards north of the station. The cross-shaft eventually came into the possession of Mr J. Lobb of Lanescot, and when the property was sold to a Mr Varcoe in 1939, the stone was donated to Tywardreath O.C.S. who had it erected in its present position in 1957.

Tywardreath had an ancient Priory to the south of the church in the valley, whose buildings were pulled down soon after the Dissolution of the monasteries in 1536. There are still many carved stones from these buildings, built into private houses in the village. Perhaps somewhere in the vicinity the head of this cross still lies, waiting to be re-discovered. The cross-head would have been either a latin cross-head with chamfered angles or a lantern cross.

Height 3ft 4 1/2ins (1.03M), width of shaft (at top) 11 3/4ft (0.30M), width of shaft (at ground level) 1ft 2ins (0.355M).

89

Tregaminion no 1
Tywardreath

WHEEL-HEADED WAYSIDE CROSS

SX 0965 5189 - Situated in the chapel yard of Tregaminion, which is 2 miles south-east of Tywardreath churchtown. Access - Unlimited.

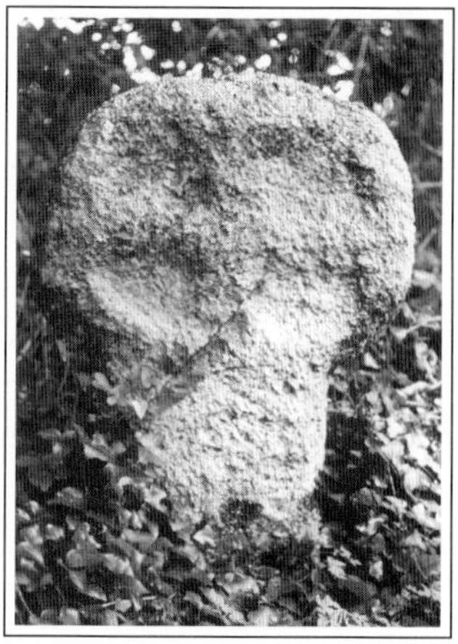

Numerous ancient crosses were removed from their original sites during the Victorian period, most being displaced with very little record of their removal, causing much of their former history to be lost. That is certainly the case with this cross, of which all we know is that it was '*removed from the roadside*'. Henderson suggested that this may have been the road outside the chapel at Tregaminion, although his reason for this assertion is not known. The Chapel of Ease at Tregaminion was built by William Rashleigh Esq. in 1815, and this wayside cross can be seen on top of the boundary hedge on the left-hand side of the chapel. The stone is cut from coarse-grained moorland granite and consists of a cross-head with a short portion of shaft, supported on an old millstone. The cross symbol in relief is formed by the positioning of four triangular depressions on the head; the reverse face is similar and the shaft is plain.

Height 3ft 0 3/4ins (0.935M), width of head 1ft 8 1/2ins (0.52M), width of shaft 1ft 1ins (0.33M), thickness 8ins (0.2M).

90

Tregaminion no 2
Tywardreath

WHEEL-HEADED WAYSIDE CROSS

SX 0966 5189 - Also in Tregaminion chapel yard. Access - Unlimited.

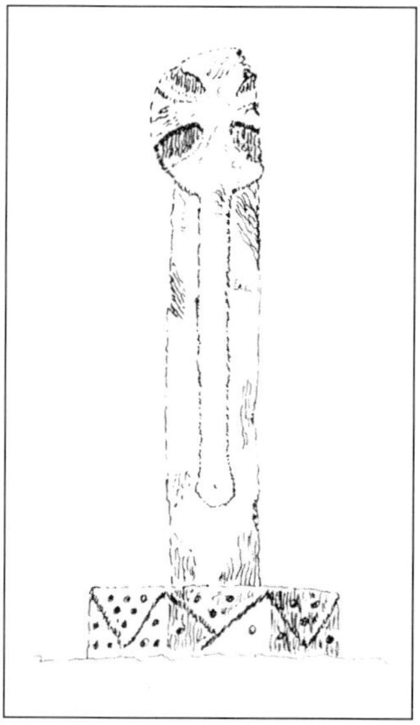

This cross was discovered in 1889 in use as a footbridge across a small stream at Milltown in the parish of Lanlivery. Soon after its discovery the stone was purchased for £5 by the monks of Buckfast Abbey in Devon, to where the monument was removed. On hearing this, the landowner, Mr William Rashleigh of Menabilly, claimed the monument and it was later brought back to Tywardreath and set up at Tregaminion.

The cross-head has been trimmed down in line with the shaft on one side, probably so that it would fit against another stone during the construction of the footbridge, and on one side the shaft is badly scarred, probably from its use as a footbridge. The cross displays limbs with widely expanded ends, the lower limb of which is extended down the shaft in low relief with incised lines, and terminates within a foot of the base-stone. The reverse face displays a similar cross, minus its extended lower limb. The octagonal base-stone was removed from Pridmouth (now known as Polridmouth), where it was in use as a pivot stone for a mill. The stone is a type of decorated millstone and is ornamented with incised zig-zag lines and small holes. The author has recorded several of these stones within the county: one at Lavethan, Blisland also supports a stone cross.

Height 6ft (1.83M), width of head 1ft 2ins (0.36M), width of shaft 1ft (0.305M), thickness 8ins (0.2M).

91

Methrose Cross, Menabilly Tywardreath

WHEEL-HEADED WAYSIDE CROSS

SX 1025 5103 - In the grounds of Menabilly Estate. Access - The monument is on private grounds, there is no public access.

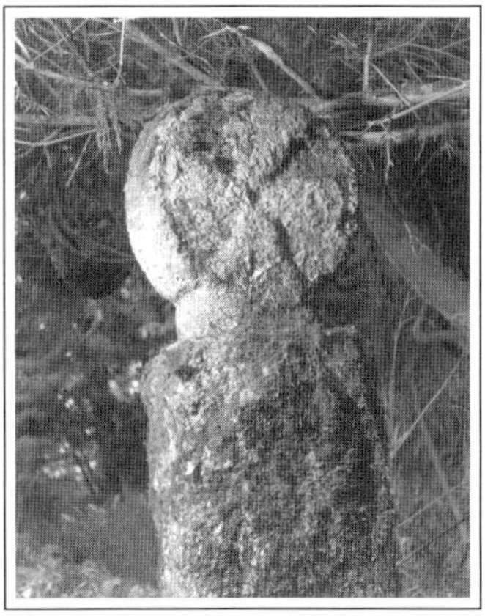

Originally, this cross marked an ancient track to Luxulyan churchtown from the farms of Carne and Methrose on the south side of the parish of Luxulyan (now part of the Saints' Way footpath). Here, at a field called 'Broom Park' at Methrose, the stone was seen during the 1880s built into the hedge. Some years later, in 1890, Mr Rashleigh had the monument removed to Menabilly and erected on a modern granite shaft.

Records suggest that the cross-base was also removed to Menabilly, although this appears to have been lost, and may in fact have never been removed from Luxulyan. The cross-head displays a plain equal-limbed cross in relief with expanded ends, with a similar cross on the reverse face enclosed in a bead. Only a short portion of cross-shaft exists, the remainder of which was probably utilised as a gatepost.

Height 1ft 7 1/2ins (0.495M), width of head 1ft 5 1/2ins (0.445M), width of shaft 9 1/2ins (0.24M), thickness 5 1/2ins (0.14M).

92

Barrs Cross, Menabilly Tywardreath

WHEEL-HEADED BOUNDARY CROSS

SX 1022 5116 - In the grounds of Menabilly House. Access - the monument is on private grounds, there is no public access.

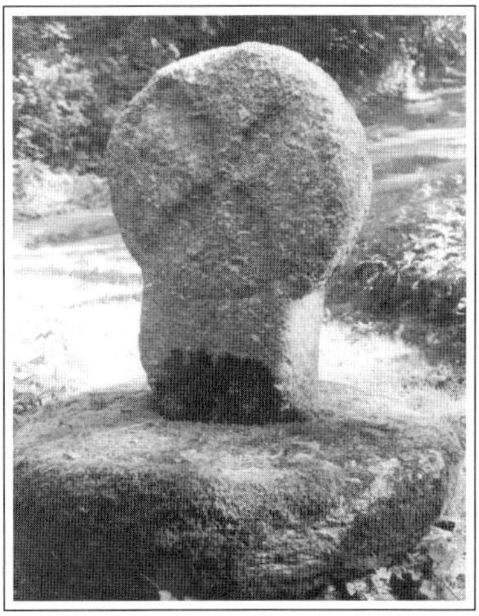

In 1896, Langdon recorded that this cross was formerly *in situ* at Milltown, marking the parish boundary between St Sampson, Golant and Lanlivery. When the cross was removed to Menabilly, William Rashleigh Esq. had a granite post set up in its place. However, this granite post is sited not at Milltown, but on the main highway between Fowey and Lostwithiel at the junction with Lantyan Lane (Grid Ref: SX 0998 5691). Here, the parishes do meet, whereas at Milltown they do not and never appear to have met. This site is only about 1/2 mile south of the hamlet of Milltown and is marked by a granite pillar, which is inscribed as the site of Barrs Cross or Barry's Cross. Moreover, a field almost opposite the site is recorded on the Tithe Map of 1839 as "Barrs Cross Meadow".

The massive cross-head sits in its original base-stone and displays a fine equal-limbed cross in relief with widely expanded ends within a narrow bead. In the centre of the cross is a small hole and on the shaft can be seen a small horizontal incised line with parallel lines running down the shaft. Unfortunately the greater part of the cross-shaft is missing and therefore the decoration is incomplete. According to the Rashleigh family, the cross is set up on the grave of Jonathan Rashleigh's favourite donkey; Mr Rashleigh used a donkey and trap to ride around the grounds of Menabilly.

Height 3ft 2ins (0.965M), width of shaft 1ft 6ins (0.46M), width of head 2ft 2ins (0.66M), thickness 9ins (0.23M), base-stone 3ft 10ins dia. (1.17M), thickness of base 10ins (0.255M).

93

Trenython Cross, Tywardreath

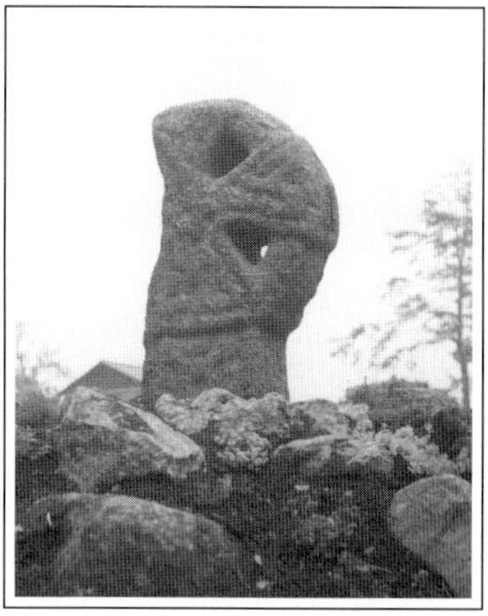

MONASTIC or CHURCHYARD CROSS

SX 1008 5410 - In the gardens of Trenython Manor which is situated 1 mile east of Tywardreath churchtown. Access - Trenython is now a Country Hotel, and the cross stands on private grounds, but access may be allowed if using the hotel's facilities.

In 1898, the damaged head and a part of the shaft of this four-holed cross was discovered by the Rt Rev W. Gott at the bottom of a dried out pond at Trenython. The Rt Rev Gott was then Bishop of Truro, and Trenython the Bishop's Palace. The remains of the cross-head stood in the grounds for many years. During this time the property changed hands several times and when the author visited Trenython in September 1986 the monument was found lying on the ground. The owner, Mr Bishop, arranged to have the cross set up on a new rockery in the gardens and this work was completed in May 1987, making the stone secure for years to come.

The cross was originally highly decorated but at some time in the past a large section of the monument was broken off including one of the horizontal limbs. Nevertheless, some of the ornamentation can still be seen, including a narrow bead running around the limbs, and containing triquetra knots. The monument is far too elaborate to have been a simple wayside or boundary cross and it is considered more probable that the stone was connected with the site of the Tywardreath Priory, which is in the valley to the south of the parish church.

Height 3ft 3ins (0.99M), width of head 1ft 7 1/2ins (0.495M), width of shaft 1ft 3ins (0.38M), thickness 8ins (0.23M).

94

Cross-head in porch wall Veryan

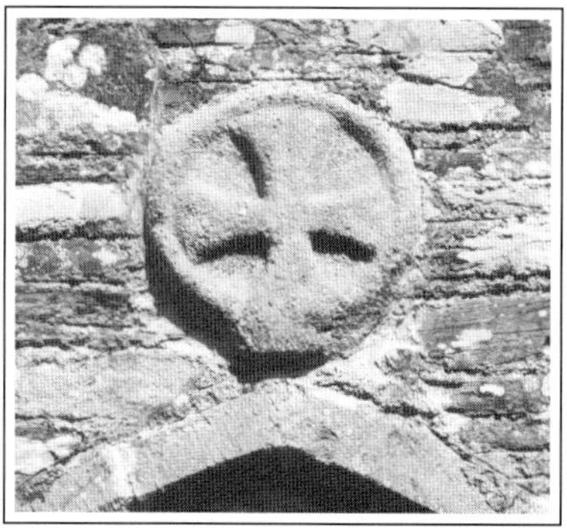

WHEEL-HEADED BOUNDARY or WAYSIDE CROSS

SW 9169 3952 - Built into the south porch of Veryan church, Veryan churchtown is situated 4 miles south of Tregony. Access - Unlimited.

It is unusual to discover a wheel-headed cross in this area of the county, since all the remaining fragments of stone crosses in Veryan parish appear to be Gothic and are latin-style crosses. The only other wheel-headed cross that exists in this area is at Gerrans (see no 38 in this guide).

This cross was first recorded in the 1920s and has been built into the external wall of the south porch, just above the archway. Mary Henderson suggested that a long piece of stone, seen built into the east side of the tower just above the drip mould, could be the missing shaft of the monument. Unfortunately, as the stone is situated near the top of the tower, it is inaccessible and will be difficult to confirm. Restoration of the church took place between 1847 and 1851 and the author considers that it was probably during this period that the cross-head was built into the porch for preservation.

The cross-head is cut from a piece of fine grained granite and displays an equal-limbed cross with expanded ends within a narrow bead. Only one inch of shaft exists, which is evidence that the cross was once a free standing monument. The monument is well preserved, although because it is built into the wall, its reverse face cannot be examined.

Diameter of cross-head 1ft 4ins (0.405M), thickness - unknown.

95

Veryan Cross Fragment
Veryan

VILLAGE CROSS

SW 9163 3958 - Situated close to the War Memorial in the centre of Veryan churchtown. Access - Unlimited.

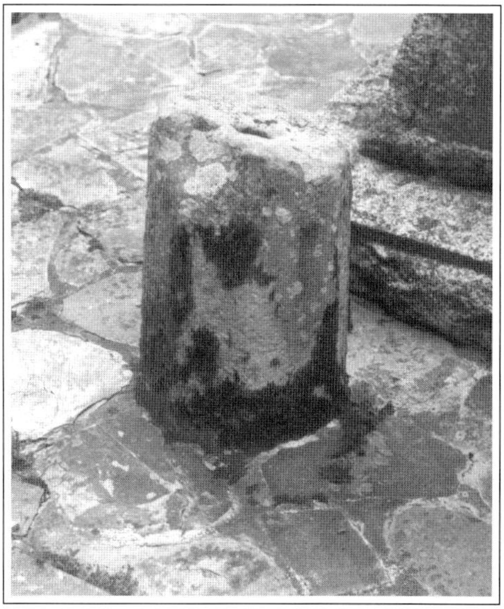

The stump of what is considered to be the original village or market cross can be seen beside the large War Memorial cross in the centre of the village, close to the parish church. There are no records of the original monument, which is thought to be *in situ*, its base-stone buried below the surround of the War Memorial.

The fragment of shaft which exists is octagonal in section and would have supported a lantern-style cross-head or latin cross. Four leaded holes in the sides of the shaft, and a two inch diameter hole remaining in the top, suggest that an iron bar may have been inserted at one stage to repair a fracture to the monument.

Height 1ft 7 1/4ins (0.49M), width 12 1/2ins (0.32M).

96

Vicarage Cross
Veryan

GOTHIC LATIN CROSS

SW 9170 3936 - Situated at the entrance to the old vicarage at Veryan churchtown. Access - Although the monument is on private ground, it can be easily viewed from the public road.

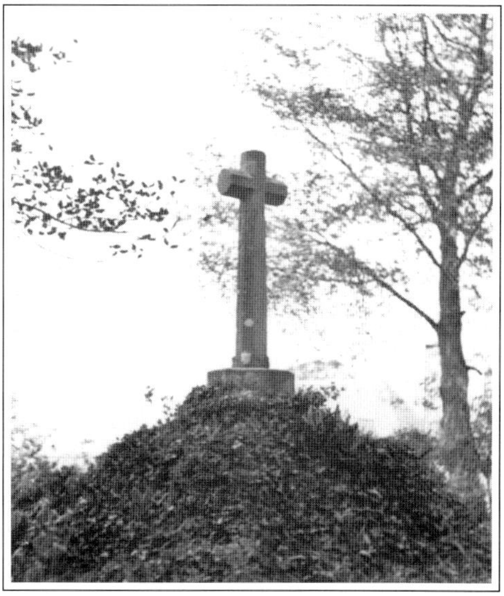

For many years the shaft of this Gothic latin cross lay in the school yard at Veryan. At the beginning of the century the stone was rescued by Canon Kempe and set up on a modern base-stone with a new cross-head. The restoration work was well executed for the base-stone is a good replica of a Gothic style stone and with its new cross-head the stones compliment each other well and are a credit to the craftsman.

The completed monument was set up on a grass bank 15 feet above the roadside close to the entrance of the old vicarage, which is situated three hundred yards south of the parish church. Today, the monument is shrouded by trees, but during the 1950s was much more visible, as seen in the photograph. The author has no knowledge of the stone's previous history, although he considers that it was most likely a wayside cross. There is documentary evidence of wayside crosses being set up in Cornwall as late as the 16th century and these would have been of the Gothic style.

Height of original shaft 3ft 71/2ins (1.105M), width of original shaft 8ins (0.2M), height of restored monument 6ft 9ins (2.057M).

97

Crossy Ann, St Wenn

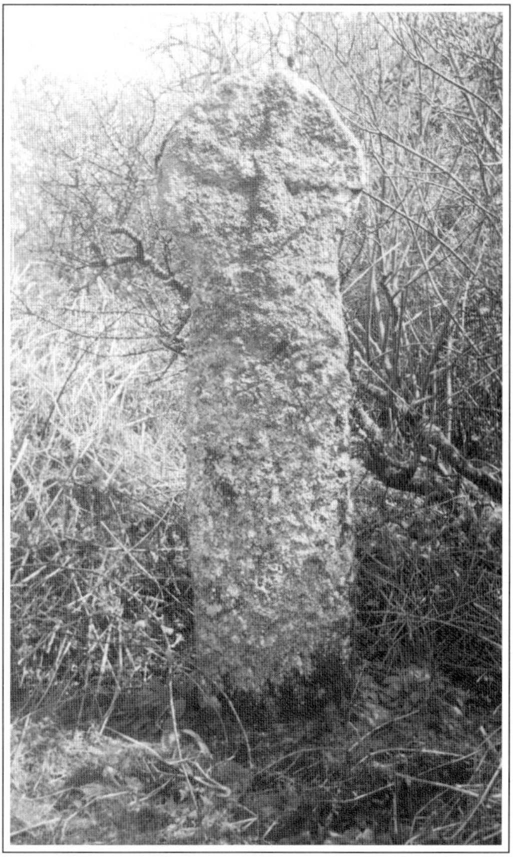

WHEEL-HEADED BOUNDARY CROSS

SW 9574 6262 - Situated on Tregonetha Downs, 3 1/2 miles east of St Columb Major, and to the west of the ancient earthworks of Castle an Dinas. Access - Tregonetha Downs is privately owned, the author is unable to ascertain whether there is any public access to the cross.

In the parish Terrier for St Columb Major in 1613, the description of the parish boundary contained a reference to this, calling it *'Ye Cross of ye hand'*. Today, the cross is still called 'Cross and Hand' or locally 'Crossy Ann'. Here, on Tregonetha Downs, this monument marks the boundary of three parishes: St Wenn, St Columb Major and Roche, and is considered to be *in situ*. The ancient stone stands in its base-stone within an overgrown thicket, in an area where the ground is undulating, making it difficult to find. A second base-stone lying 100 yards to the north-west (see no 19 in this guide), marks the continuation of the St Columb Major/St Wenn boundary at NGR SW 9566 6266. The name 'Cross and Hand' is said to derive from the fact that the outline of an incised hand could be discerned upon the upper segment of the cross-head. It was supposed to represent the hand of God. This decoration cannot now be seen and historians have suggested that the monument which stood in the second base-stone on the Downs was in fact the cross displaying the hand, and that when this cross was lost or destroyed, the existing cross adopted its name. Another cross known as 'Cross and Hand' is recorded at Batcombe Down in the county of Dorset. The monument displays a parallel-limbed cross, which is crudely executed and has crooked limbs of irregular sizes; the reverse face has a similar cross on it. The plain shaft has an entasis on both sides and is mortice-jointed into an oval base-stone.

Height 5ft 11ins (1.8M), width of head 1ft 11ins (0.585M), width of shaft (at neck) 1ft 3ins (0.38M), width of shaft (at base) 1ft 5 1/2ins (0.445M), thickness 8ins to 10ins (0.2M to 0.255M).

98

Rostigan Cross-shaft, St Wenn

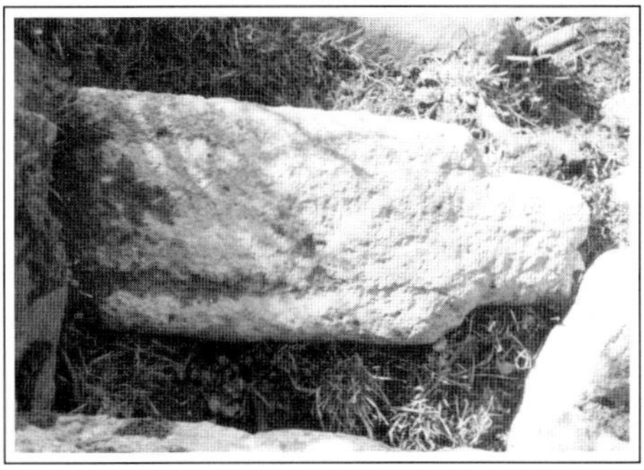

SHAFT OF WHEEL-HEADED BOUNDARY CROSS

SW 9718 6468 - On a footpath 1/4 mile south-east of St Wenn parish church. Access Unlimited.

In 1601, the parish Terrier for St Wenn mentioned the site of a stone cross as a boundstone marking the glebe. *'The Glebe is bounded by Rechigian Crose in the highway till it cometh to Polgrene (Braban's land)....'*. The author on reading this decided to search for this ancient monument and was surprisingly rewarded by discovering the lower portion of cross-shaft, built into a stile, at a point where the church path intersects the boundary of the glebe. It had been used as the second step on the field side of a stile and consisted of the lower section of shaft and the tenon, with a bead running up each side. The head, upper portion of shaft and the base-stone remain missing despite a systematic search of the surrounding area. The stile appears to be on the original boundary of the glebe and the land is still owned by Glebe Farm, in the churchtown. If the monument originally stood by the stile it may have held a dual function as both a medieval guide post marking the church path and also the boundary of the glebe. The field where the stile is situated and the adjoining field to the east are known as 'Cross Park' and 'Higher Cross Park'; on the Tithe Apportionment map of 1841, the field on the opposite side of the road is also known as 'Cross Park'.

Length 2ft 5 1/2ins (0.75M), width 1ft (0.305M), thickness 7 1/2ins (0.19M).

99

Tregurtha Cross-head St Wenn

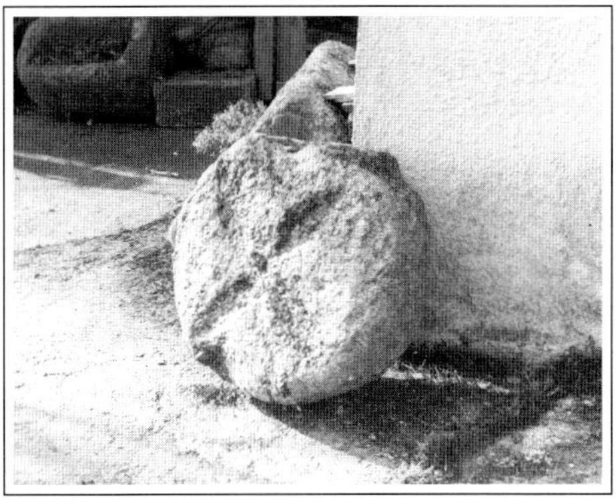

WHEEL-HEADED WAYSIDE or BOUNDARY CROSS

SW 9573 6441 - Situated at Tregurtha Farm, St Wenn. Tregurtha lies 3/4 mile south-west of St Wenn churchtown. Access - The stone is on private grounds, there is no public access.

In December 1988, the author was invited to examine a stone which had been discovered at Tregurtha Farm while a drainage ditch was being cleared out. The stone had been known to Mr Bennalick, the owner, for many years but had never been closely examined until then.

The granite cross-head displays an equal-limbed cross with widely expanded ends on both faces, one face of which has been disfigured by a socket-type hole. This appears to have been used as a pivot for some kind of machine. It is not known where the stone originated, although a church path still crosses the fields of Tregurtha Farm from the village of Tregonetha, and the cross may have once marked this route. The author hopes that in the future this ancient cross may be restored and re-erected.

Height 1ft 8ins (0.508M), width 1ft 9 1/2ins (0.545M), thickness 6 1/2ins to 7 1/2ins (0.165M to 0.19M).

100

Rectory Cross
Withiel

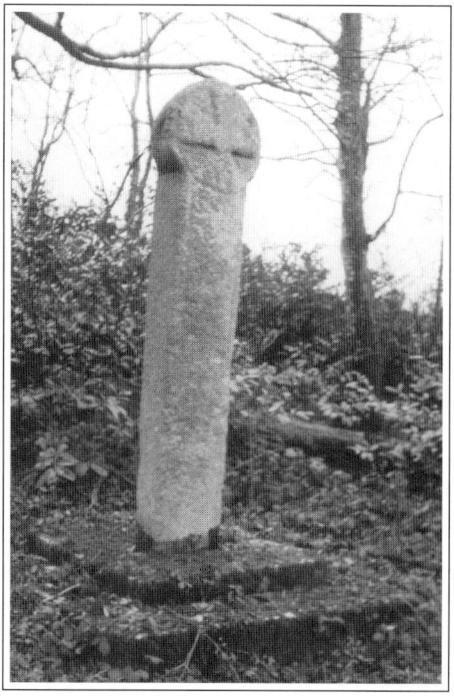

WHEEL-HEADED WAYSIDE or BOUNDARY CROSS

SW 9931 6525 - Situated in the grounds of the Old Rectory at Withiel. Withiel churchtown lies 6 miles west of Bodmin. Access - The cross is on private ground, there is no public access.

This fine example of a wayside cross was removed from the roadside close to the rectory entrance prior to 1858 and was re-erected on a stepped base in the rectory gardens. The monument originally stood on the route to the parish church, although in the author's opinion, being so close to the church, its function is unclear. It may have been set up as a wayside cross or to mark the boundary of glebe land. On the Tithe Apportionment map of 1841, the field bordering the rectory gardens on the south side was known as 'Cross Park' and is in close proximity to the original site.

The cross is a very well proportioned monument displaying a Greek style cross in relief with the lower limb expanded to almost the full width of the shaft. The cross is enclosed by a narrow bead which continues down both sides of the plain shaft. There is no record of whether the cross-base existed at the time of the removal of the monument to the rectory grounds. In 1896, Langdon noted that a cross-base was built into the churchyard path, probably the original base, but today the stone cannot be found and may be buried below the existing path level.

Height 7ft 5 1/2ins (2.275M), width of head 1ft 10 1/2ins (0.57M), width of shaft 1ft 1ins (0.33M), thickness 8ins to 10ins (0.215M to 0.265M).

101

Inches Cross
Withiel

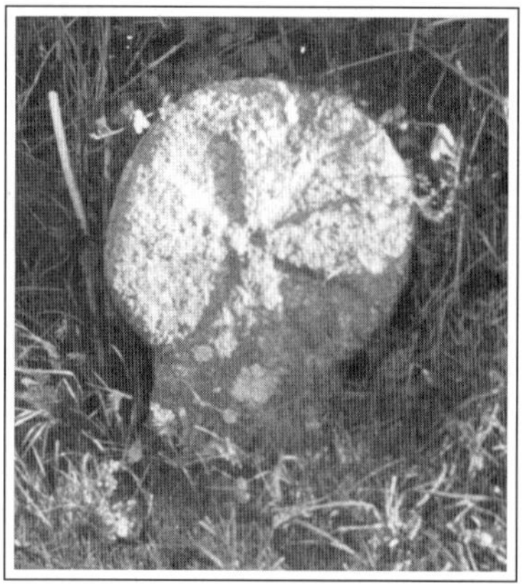

WHEEL-HEADED WAYSIDE CROSS

SW 9951 6370 - Situated 1 1/4 miles due south of the parish church. Access - Unlimited.

This wheel-headed cross stands beside a hedge close to the roadside near the farm of Inches, hence its name. The cross is recorded as being deeply buried and therefore may be a much taller monument than it appears now. No base-stone can be identified at the site but the cross is considered to be *in situ*, marking the direct route from Roche north to Withiel churchtown.

The stone displays a similar cross to the one shown on the Rectory Cross at Withiel but in faint relief. The lower limb is expanded to the full width of the shaft and the reverse face resembles it. There is no bead either around the cross-head or down the shaft of the monument, and the ends of the limbs extend to the edge of the stone.

Height 2ft 9ins (0.84M), width of head 2ft 1 1/2ins (0.65M), width of shaft 1ft 3ins (0.38M), thickness 9ins (0.23M).

5 - APPENDIX

i - LIST OF STONES NOT FEATURED IN THIS GUIDE

The following list gives a brief reference to the many fragments of crosses not featured in this guide. The majority are cross-bases, although some are stones of doubtful origin and are difficult to authenticate: they are therefore recorded as "possibles".

Trethurgy, St Austell SX 0325 5545 POSSIBLE GOTHIC CROSS-SHAFT
There is no public access, the stone stands on private ground. The granite shaft is octagonal in section and tapers slightly. It was discovered buried in the garden of the property and measures just over 2 feet in length.

Trevithick East, St Columb Major SW 9330 6382 POSSIBLE CROSS-BASE
There is no public access, the stone stands on private ground. Henderson first recorded this stone with a socket cut through it. The stone is one of several worked stones at the property.

Tregamere, St Columb Major SW 9225 6444 POSSIBLE CROSS-BASE
Unlimited public access: this stone stands beside the old Wadebridge to St Columb Major road. The stone is known as the country goal and is used in the ancient game of Hurling. Henderson recorded it as a cross-base, although in the author's opinion the socket is too shallow.

Beneath the tower arch, St Columb Major SW 9130 6366 CROSS SLAB/COFFIN SLAB
Unlimited public access, this granite slab is fixed below the tower arch at St Columb Major church, along with a coffin slab. This slab has a wheel cross in relief carved on it.

Cross Mound, St Columb Minor SW 8394 6233 GOTHIC CROSS-BASE
There is no public access, though the base-stone lies in a private garden and can easily be viewed from the public pavement. The stone at one time stood on a mound of grass in the street and was locally known as 'Cross Mound'.

Penrose, St Columb Minor SW 8441 6292 GOTHIC CROSS-BASE
Unlimited public access: the stone stands beside a public footpath. The stone stands on the parish boundary between St Columb Minor and Colan, beside a track which leads from Penrose to Tregustick.

Penpoll Cross, Crantock SW 7940 6056 MODERN CROSS ON AN ANCIENT BASE
Unlimited public access. The Gothic style base-stone marked an ancient track across the Gannel to Crantock church. Earlier this century a modern cross was set up on the base-stone.

West Pentire, Crantock SW 7766 6063 GOTHIC CROSS-BASE
There is no public access: the stone is on private ground. The large cross-base stands in the front garden at Pentire Manor House and would have originally supported an octagonal sectioned Latin cross.

Trerew Farm, Crantock SW 8129 5827 CROSS-BASE
There is no public access: the cross stands on private ground. The cross-base was first recorded by Henderson in the 1920s and it is suggested that it supported a cross which marked the church path to Crantock church.

Trevemper, Crantock SW 8152 5973 CROSS-BASE
Unlimited public access. The stone stands on a triangular piece of ground on a road junction of the A3075 and a minor road west to Crantock churchtown. Its round mortice suggests that it may not be authentic.

Bosillian, Creed with Grampound SW 9424 4788 POSSIBLE GOTHIC CROSS-BASE
Unlimited public access: the stone stands beside a lane near Bosillian Farm. The base is cut from Pentewan stone and has been used as a Hurling goal for many years.

At theMarket Cross, Creed with Grampound SW 9360 4831 POSSIBLE GOTHIC CROSS-BASE
Unlimited public access: the stone stands beside the public highway. This socket stone, recorded as a cross-base, is also cut from Pentewan stone and is identical to the Bosillian stone. In the author's opinion they may never have been cross-bases but the town and country goals for the ancient game of Hurling.

Trevillick, Creed with Grampound SW 9387 4884 CROSS-BASE
Although set up high on a private hedge, the stone can be viewed from the public highway, which runs north from St Nun's Chapel towards Trevillick Farm. This cross-base is much earlier than the other remaining Gothic bases in this area and is cut from granite.

Heligan, St Ewe SW 9991 4640 GOTHIC GABLE CROSS
The stone stands on private property, and there is no public access. This small granite gable cross, which is octagonal in section, stands close to the Bokiddick Cross (see no 32 in this guide). Its former history is unknown.

Churchtown, St Goran SW 9993 4228 POSSIBLE GOTHIC CROSS-SHAFT
Unlimited public access. The granite shaft stands on a raised piece of ground close to the parish church. The shaft is octagonal in section and may have once been the village cross.

Mission Church, Kea SW 8444 4172 GABLE CROSS
There is public access when the church is unlocked. The small granite gable cross lies close to the font. It was probably originally fixed to the old parish church at Kea, and was possibly the cross that was fixed to the missing pinnacle of the church tower.

Guildhall Lane, Lanlivery with Lostwithiel SX 1036 5976 POSSIBLE BASE-STONE
Unlimited public access: the lane is a public byway. According to a guide book on Lostwithiel, this large oval granite slab may be the original base-stone of the town's market cross. The stone is set into the ground at a bend in the lane.

Churchyard, St Mawgan in Pydar SW 8723 6595 GOTHIC CROSS-BASE
Unlimited public access. The stone now stands on the south-west side of the tower and has been converted into a boot scraper. It formerly stood by the church porch and was rescued in 1942, from a cottage which was demolished prior to the building of the aerodrome.

Churchyard, St Mawgan in Pydar SW 8727 6593 CROSS-BASE
Unlimited public access. The cross-base stands on the left-hand side of the path leading to the church from the lychgate. Again, this base-stone was rescued at the time of building the aerodrome.

At Lanherne, St Mawgan in Pydar SW 8717 6591 GOTHIC CROSS-HEAD.
Within the nuns' private graveyard, there is a small Gothic latin cross, supported on a classical plinth and stepped-base. There is no public access. It was allegedly presented to the Convent by Colonel Ryves of Wurdwan in St Mawgan. The cross displays sculptured figures of the Crucifixion on one face and the Virgin Mary and Child on the other.

Lower Lodge Cottage, St Mawgan in Pydar CARVED CRUCIFIX.
On the wall of this cottage, just below the roof in a blocked-up window recess can be seen a carved Crucifix of unknown origin. Its appearance suggests that it may be relatively modern. It can be viewed from the public road.

Churchyard, St Mewan SX 9982 5185 GOTHIC CROSS-BASE
Unlimited public access. The base stone lies on a grass bank close to the western side of the church. It is a large square granite stone with a square socket in it. A second round shaped stone with a round mortice lies nearby, but the author is not convinced that it was used to support a cross.

Trewithen, Probus SW 9129 4752 GOTHIC CROSS-BASE
There is no public access: the stone stands on private property. The base-stone was rescued in the 1920s by Mr G.H. Johnstone of Trewithen from the Crown Inn, St. Ewe, where it was used for washing beer bottles. (See no 33 in this guide).

Churchyard, St Stephen in Brannel SW 9449 5331 CROSS-BASE
Unlimited public access. This base-stone is utilised as a plant container on the south side of the churchyard. The shrub has now completely overwhelmed this ancient stone, making examination of it very difficult.

ii - MODERN CROSSES

There is an increasing number of modern replica wayside crosses being set up around the county. Because most are sensitively executed and positioned, there is a concern that some will be mistaken for genuine ancient crosses. In a few cases an ageing process is applied by stonemasons to give the monument an appearance of antiquity. It is the author's opinion that they should at least be dated to save confusion in future years. The symbol of the cross in Cornwall is increasingly being seen as not only a religious symbol, but also a cultural symbol. His file on modern replicas is growing all the time!

Since 1999, many parishes in both Cornwall and Devon have initiated projects to erect stone crosses for the millennium. There are new crosses at Liskeard, Helston, St Dennis and Newquay, to name but a few. During March 2002, a very large modern boundary cross was carved by stonemasons at the De Lank granite quarry at St Breward, and erected at Bodmin.

Another area where identifying ancient crosses may become more difficult is in our parish churchyards. Local monumental masons have for many years tried to match their skills against those of the medieval craftsman, so that today there are many modern copies of wayside and churchyard crosses in local churchyards and cemeteries. There are several good examples in Lelant cemetery as well as St Levan and St Columb Minor.

There is documentary evidence of many crosses which once existed in the county, this list only represents a few of the monuments which have been lost.

Mawla Cross, St Agnes
This cross was mentioned as a boundary stone for the manor of Tywarnhayle in 1617. Part of the bounds read, 'from the water by Stencoose and Mola Cross and Mola Lane End and so down to Melgisey Water.....'.

Trevenson Cross-base, St Columb Minor
This cross-base formerly stood beside a public footpath that runs from Trevenson Hill to Treloggan Lane. The stone stood at SW 8387 6172, but was reported missing in 2001, despite a thorough search.

Gargus, Tregonjohn and Tregidgeo, Creed with Grampound
Mary Henderson recorded that cross-bases once existed at all three of these sites. For further information, see Miss Henderson's manuscript in the Courtney Library, at the County Museum.

White Cross, St Enoder with Mitchell
The village of Whitecross stands beside the A392 highway between St Columb Road and Newquay. Here the parishes of St Enoder with Mitchell, St Columb Major and Colan meet. Field names here suggest the site of a boundary cross.

Trevellion Lane End, Luxulyan
Charles Henderson illustrated this cross-shaft in the *Western Morning News* newspaper in February 1924; at this time it was in use as a gatepost. In 1974, it was re-discovered by the landowner Mr Hoskin and recorded by Mary henderson, but has since been lost again!

White Cross, St Mewan
According to Charles Henderson, a White Cross is mentioned in the bounds of Burngullow Common which read, '...by Burngulloe lane end at a place or stone called White Crosse that divideth the lands of Mr Tanner and Burngulloe and from there direct North to a rock called Carrackangoge about half a myle from White Crosse..'.

Higher Mount Farm, Perranzabuloe
Mary Henderson recorded a portion of octagonal cross-shaft in use as a gatepost on the right-handed side of the road from Perranzabuloe to Cubert at Grid Ref. SW 7790 5574. Since the first edition of this book the stone has been removed.

Carvossa Cross, Probus
The parish of Probus formerly had a Sanctuary which extended beyond the four walls of the church. One of its boundaries was marked by Carvossa Cross (see no 79 in this guide). Baird recorded a stump of stone by the wastral at Carvossa which he suggested was the remains of the cross, although today it is not visible.

Trebilcock, Trenower, and Tregonhay, Roche
In his 1937 publication, *A Story of the parish of Roche*, Cresswell Payne recorded the existence of three cross-bases in the parish with quite detailed directions, yet today not one survives.

Barn, Ruan Lanihorne
Charles Henderson believed that the capstone of a buttress outside the garden doorway was a mutilated fragment of a Celtic cross.

Rostigan, St Wenn
The lower part of this boundary cross is in use as a step to a stile (see no 98 in this guide), but the cross-head and the remainder of the shaft are still missing and probably buried in a nearby hedge.

iv - CHRONOLOGY OF RECENT CROSS DISCOVERIES IN CORNWALL

March 1984*	St Just in Penwith	LATIN CROSS	SW 3524 3185
August 1984	Trevilley, Sennen	CROSS-BASE	SW 3570 2464
April 1984*	Hendra, Menheniot	WHEEL CROSS	SX 2697 6545
December 1986*	Tredinnick, St. Breock	CROSS-HEAD	SW 9722 7212
August 1987	Trelights, St. Endellion	CROSS-BASE	SW 9902 7876
April 1988*	Penrose, Wendron	CROSS FRAGMENT	SW 6413 2576
1988*	Castle Site, Tintagel	TWO STONES DISPLAYING CROSSES	
October 1988	Tregonning, Luxulyan	CROSS-HEAD	SX 0539 5702
December 1988*	Tregurtha, St. Wenn	CROSS-HEAD	SW 9586 6447
April 1989*	Trevadlock, Lewannick	GOTHIC CROSS-HEAD	SX 2651 7902
February 1989	Rostigan, St. Wenn	CROSS-SHAFT	SW 9718 6468
May 1989	Tregrylls, Lesnewth	LATIN CROSS	SX 1269 8944
January 1990	Lower Kernick, Helland	CROSS-BASE	SX 0848 7130
September 1990	Menawink, Lanlivery	WHEEL CROSS	SX 0711 5958
July 1991	Lamorrick, Lanivet	WHEEL CROSS	SX 0358 6460
June 1993	High Cross, Constantine	WHEEL CROSS	SW 7510 2933
June 1994	Trefranck, St Clether	WHEEL CROSS	SX 2037 8494
August 1995	North Petherwin Church	LATIN GABLE CROSS	SX 2820 8961
March 1997	Churchyard St Ervan	GOTHIC CROSS-BASE	SW 8918 7027
September 1998	Gwealavellan, Camborne	WHEEL CROSS	SW 6004 4189
April 1999	Higher Fawton, St Neot	LATIN CROSS	Removed to Devonshire
May 2000	Castallack, Paul	CROSS-BASE	SW 4515 2527
July 2002*	St Clether	WHEEL CROSS	No access

* Indicates crosses that are on private ground with no public access at present, other monuments recorded here may be on private ground but are beside public footpaths or rights of way.

ABACUS	A collar-like disc around the neck of a stone cross.
BEAD	A narrow moulding of semi-circular section, seen around the head and down the sides of many Cornish crosses.
BENCHMARK	Broad arrow symbol carved on stone by surveyors to mark reference point of levels, usually cut by Ordnance Survey.
BOSS	Carved or sculptured circular projection, which is normally half round.
CHAMFERED	A bevelled edge running down the shaft of a monument.
CROSS-CROSSLET	An equal-limbed cross, with additional crosses formed on each limb.
CUSPS	Projecting point between two arcs in Gothic tracery or in the holes of a four-holed cross.
DISC HEADED	This is another name for a round or wheel head of a cross.
ENTASIS	Slight convexity of a column or shaft, provided to correct the visual illusion of concavity.
EXPANDED LIMBS	Limbs that are not of a uniform width, but wider at the ends than at the centre.
FOLIATED	Decoration which is leaf-like in appearance.
GLEBE	Land attached to the parish church.
INCISED CROSS	A cross cut into a piece of material, rather than being carved in relief.
INTERLACE WORK	Decoration consisting of cords in a plaited form.
MINUSCULES	7th century script in small letters instead of capitals (Anglo Saxon).
MONOLITH	Single large block or pillar of stone.
MORTICE	Hole or socket cut into a base-stone to receive a tenon of a cross.
OGHAM (OGAM)	British/Irish alphabet consisting of straight lines across, or either side of a continuous line.
PEDESTAL	Raised base-stone or support for a cross.

PLINTH	Similar to a pedestal, a support or base-stone for a monument.
PROJECTIONS	Protrusions at the neck or on the head of a wheel-headed cross.
REBATED	In a few cases, instead of a bead around the head and shaft of a cross, a similar effect is produced by reducing the thickness on the edge of the monument.
RELIEF	A method of carving,where the design stands out from the surface in a raised position.
RELIQUARY	A receptacle for the placing of relics.
RING	The segment of stone joining adjacent limbs of a four-holed cross.
TENON	Projecting section of stone at the bottom of a cross-shaft to fit into a corresponding socket (mortice) in a base-stone.
TREFOIL HOLES	Holes in the shape of a three-lobed leaf.
TREQUETRA KNOTS	Symmetrical decoration formed from three interlaced arcs.

vi - BIBLIOGRAPHY

BORLASE, W. — *Antiquities Historical and Monumental of the County of Cornwall* 1754.

RANDOLPH, F.C.H. — *Specimens of Ancient Cornish Crosses and Fonts* 1850.

BLIGHT J. T. — Personal sketch books at the Morrab Library, Penzance.

BLIGHT J.T. — *Ancient Crosses and Antiquities of West Cornwall* 1856.

BLIGHT J.T. — *Ancient Crosses and Antiguities of East Cornwall* 1858.

POLSUE, J. — *A Parochial History of Cornwall* in four volumes, 1867, 1868, 1870 and 1872.

IAGO REV W. — Many papers on Crosses and inscribed stones published in various *Royal Institution of Cornwall* Journals.

LANGDON Arthur G. and ROMILLY ALLEN J. — 'The Early Christian Monuments of Cornwall', a paper published by the *British Archaeological Association* 1888.

LANGDON Arthur G. 'The Ornament on the Early Crosses of Cornwall', a paper published in the *Royal Institution of Cornwall Journal* Vol. X part 1. May 1890 p. 33-96.

LANGDON Arthur G. *Old Cornish Crosses* 1896 (reprinted 1988).

LANGDON Arthur G. 'Early Christian Monuments' published in the *Victoria County History of Cornwall* 1906 Vol. 1

LANGDON Arthur G. Collection of additional drawings dated between 1894 and 1909, CourtneyLibrary, Royal Institutioin of Cornwall, Truro.

WILLS, S.J. Personal notebooks and mss in the Courtney Library, Royal Institution of Cornwall, Truro.

HENDERSON, C.G. Notes for a Supplement to A.G. Langdon's 'Old Cornish Crosses' 1930, housed in the Courtney Library Royal Institution of Cornwall, Truro.

HENDERSON C.G. 'Missing Cornish Crosses', a paper published in the *Old Cornwall* Vol 1. No. 12 Winter 1930 p. 6.

HENDERSON C.G. 'Cornish Crosses after Langdon's Day' in *Essays in Cornish History* 1935, p. 193-196.

PAYNE, Cresswell G.H. *A Story of the parish of Roche* 1937.

DEXTER T.F.G. & H. *Cornish Crosses, Christian and Pagan* 1938.

ELLIS G.E. 'Cornish Crosses', published in the *Devon & Cornwall Notes & Queries*, between 1952 and 1968.

BAIRD Major R.D. & LADY WHITE *Cornish Crosses* 1961, typed manuscript at the Courtney Library at the Royal Institution of Cornwall, Truro.

ROWE L. *Granite Crosses of West Cornwall* 1973.

HENDERSON M. *A Survey of Ancient Crosses of Cornwall* 1952 - 1983. A four volume, 1091 page manuscript accompanied by one volume of illustrations by L. Rowe. in the Courtney Library at the Royal Institution of Cornwall, Truro.

OKASHA E. *Corpus of Early Christian Inscribed Stones of South-west Britain* 1993.

THOMAS C. *And shall those mute stones speak* 1994.

LANGDON Andrew G. 'The Renovation of Truro's High Cross' *Old Cornwall* Spring 1989 p 406-9.

LANGDON Andrew G. *Stone Crosses in North Cornwall* 1992.

LANGDON Andrew G. *Stone Crosses in Mid Cornwall* 1994.

LANGDON Andrew G. *Stone Crosses in East Cornwall* 1996.

LANGDON Andrew G. *Stone Crosses in North Cornwall*, 2nd. Edition 1996.

LANGDON Andrew G. *An addendum to Arthur G. Langdon's Old Cornish Crosses 1896 - 1996*. Cornwall Archaeological Unit 1996.

LANGDON Andrew G. *Stone Crosses in West Penwith*, 1997.

LANGDON Andrew G. *Stone Crosses in West Cornwall*, 1999.

LANGDON Andrew G. 'Boundstone or Cross?' *Old Cornwall* Spring 2002 p29-37.

LANGDON Andrew G. Notes on Cornish Crosses in various Old Cornwall Society Journals, Vol.X, XI and XII, 1986 onwards.

PRESTON-JONES A. *The Nancor Cross, Grampound - The Restoration of a Vandalised Monument*, Cornwall Archaeological Unit, May 1996.

PRESTON-JONES A. and LANGDON A. *Restoration and Relocation of the Trevalsa Cross, St Allen*, Cornwall Archaeological Unit 1997.

no 36 Trelissick Garden, Feock.

On Friday 11th October 2002, the wheel-headed cross in the grounds of Trelissick Gardens was re-positioned approximately three metres north-west of its former site for health and safety reasons and to improve presentation.

The work involved sliding the cross, complete with its base-stone across to its new position with the help of a Tirfor hand winch. A concrete sub-base was provided at the new site, prior to the cross being moved, to prevent subsidence.

The project was organised and executed by Mr Barry Champion, Head Gardener for the National Trust at Trelissick, with assistance from assistant gardeners Dick Couch and Richard Bouch. The event was recorded by the author. (see future *Old Cornwall* journal for a complete report).

no 75 Neeham Cross-base, Newlyn East.

On Friday 27th September 2002, Mr Harold Phillips started carving the new wayside cross which is to be erected on the Neeham cross-base, as part of the Newlyn East parish council Millennium and Golden Jubilee celebrations.

On Saturday 12th October 2000, Mr Phillips completed the carving of the Neeham Cross, and arrangements are now under way to have the monument erected at Newlyn East on the ancient cross-base.